Corrective Reading

SRA
Skill Applications

Workbook

Decoding C

A Direct Instruction Program

Siegfried Engelmann

Gary Johnson

Linda Carnine

Linda Meyer

Mc
Graw
Hill
Education

Cover Photo: ©Pixtal/age Fotostock

MHEonline.com

Send all inquiries to:
McGraw-Hill Education
8787 Orion Place
Columbus, OH 43240

ISBN: 978-0-07-611239-5
MHID: 0-07-611239-X

Printed in the United States of America.

21 22 23 QVS 20 19 18 17

Errors

1

1. Where did Bert work? _____

2. a. Was Bert happy at work? _____

   b. How would you know? _____

   _____

3. Who came to the shop for an anchor chain? _____

4. What did Shirley do for a living?

   _____

5. How much did the chain cost? _____

6. Did Shirley pay for the chain or take the chain on account? _____

7. What does "on account" mean?

   _____

8. Where was Shirley taking Bert? _____

9. Was Bert stout? _____

10. **Here are three things that happened in the story.**

    Put the number 1 next to the first thing that happened.

    Put the number 2 next to the second thing that happened.

    Put the number 3 next to the third thing that happened.

    _____ Bert tried to pick up the chain.

    _____ People came to the shop to buy things.

    _____ Shirley took the chain down the stairs.

2 **Fill in each blank using a word in the box.**

churned	stout	ail
perch	grouch	strain

1. Gina was very big and _____.

2. He _____ his soup until it was all stirred.

3. The pond had some _____ swimming in it.

3 **Write the parts for each word.**

1. sailed   = _____sail_____ + _____ed_____

2. painting = _____ + _____

3. brightness = _____ + _____

4. slowest = _____ + _____

Errors

1

1. Name two things wrong with Shirley's boat.

   _____

   _____

2. What did Bert think of Shirley's boat?

   _____

3. Did Bert know what Shirley meant when she said, "Run up the main sail"? _____

4. What did Shirley mean when she said, "Run up the main sail"?

   _____

5. Why did Bert feel sick?

   _____

6. How high did the water get in the hold?

   _____

7. How deep was the water in the hold when Bert stopped bailing?

   _____

8. What happened to make the boat begin to flounder?

   _____

9. Did Shirley hear Bert's call? _____

10. Why was Bert's call faint? _____

    _____

2 Fill in each blank using a word in the box.

sound	stern	faint
hull	floundered	ail

1. The boat was _____. It didn't leak.

2. The dog _____ on the slippery ice.

3. The writing was too _____ to read.

3 Write the parts for each word.

1. soundest   =   _____sound_____   +   _____est_____

2. floundering   =   _____   +   _____

3. remained   =   _____   +   _____

4. stoutness   =   _____   +   _____

1

1. How did Bert end up in the middle of the surf? _____

_____

2. Who said hello to Bert? _____

3. What did the surfer mean when he told Bert to "keep the faith"?

_____

4. What did the surfer want Bert to think about? _____

_____

5. What did Bert see in the water? _____

6. What did the surfer tell Bert to do if he didn't like being in the surf?

_____

7. What did the surfer think Bert needed when the shark touched Bert's foot?

_____

2 **Fill in each blank using a word in the box.**

flounder	shouted	fret
faint	flailed	swirled

1. We went fishing and caught a big _____.

2. The swimmer _____ her arms.

3. Cream _____ around his coffee.

3 **Write the parts for each word.**

1. starting = _____ + _____

2. surfer = _____ + _____

3. swirled = _____ + _____

4. faintness = _____ + _____

1

1. At the beginning of the story, where were Bert and the surfer?

   _____

2. a. Did the surfer make Bert stop worrying? _____

   b. How do you know? _____

3. What would the sharks have done if Bert made loud noises?

   _____

4. Who came to the aid of Bert and the surfer? _____

5. What kind of craft did Shirley have? _____

6. **Here are some things that happened after Bert spotted Shirley's craft.**

   Number the things 1, 2, 3, and 4 to show the order in which they happened.

   _____ Bert wailed about being in the surf.

   _____ Bert bailed with a pail.

   _____ Shirley wailed, "Ahoy."

   _____ Bert climbed over a rail.

7. What would the surfer not do? _____

8. What did Shirley go to sea to do? _____

9. What did Shirley think would change Bert's mind?

   _____

2 **Fill in each blank using a word in the box.**

perched	wail	survived
flail	strain	fret

1. The baby was hungry and began to _____ in a loud voice.

2. The pigeons _____ on top of the building.

3. José _____ the shark's attack.

1

1. What was the pail of little fish used for? _____

2. What happened to Bert when he jerked on the fishing pole?

   _____

3. What did Shirley say fishing was more fun than?

   _____

4. What did the surfer and Shirley eat that night? _____

5. What did Bert do all night? _____

6. What did the termites eat first? _____

7. Why did Bert fall into a hole filled with flounder? _____

8. What did Shirley hope? _____

   _____

2 **Fill in each blank using a word in the box.**

flounder	serious	termites
suddenly	tiller	perch

1. Libby used the _____ and turned the boat around.

2. Jolene blew the balloon up until it _____ burst.

3. The _____ ate holes in our new porch.

3 **Write the parts for each word.**

1. surrounding = _____ + _____

2. grounded = _____ + _____

3. hardness = _____ + _____

4. suddenly = _____ + _____

8   *Lesson 5*

Errors

1

1. Who was the race between? _____

2. a. Who did Bert think would win the race? _____

   b. How do you know?

   _____

3. **Here are some things the termites had eaten.**

   Number them 1, 2, 3, and 4 in the order they were eaten.

   _____ hammer

   _____ deck chair

   _____ top of the mast

   _____ tiller

4. Why did Shirley want to turn toward the shore? _____

   _____

   _____

5. Where would Bert like to have been? _____

6. Why didn't the surfer like his beach? _____

   _____

7. Why did Shirley think there was a leak in the hull?

   _____

8. Why did Bert go down the stairs?

   _____

9. How did Bert feel when the hammer broke?

   _____

10. Where did Bert end up when the boat came aground next to the dock?

    _____

2   **Fill in each blank using a word in the box.**

collapsed	strain	craft
wailed	serious	survived

1. Those termites ate our house until it _____.

2. Rosa threw away her raft and built a new _____.

3. The little boy fell down and _____ in pain.

Lesson 7

1. a. Was the surfboard made of wood? _____

 b. How did it get broken? _____

2. What job did Bert want to have? _____

3. Did Shirley think Bert's job was fun? _____

4. What kind of fish did the surfer catch? _____

5. Why did Shirley ask the surfer, "Are there always shad around here?"

 Draw a line under the fact that tells why.

 Shirley likes to talk to the surfer.

 Shirley doesn't like shad.

 Shirley has a plan.

6. What does "The water is lousy with shad" mean?

 _____

7. What did Bert mean when he said, "This water is lousy—period"?

 _____

8. Shirley had a plan. Who did she think it would make happy?

 _____

9. What do you think Shirley's plan was?

 _____

 _____

2 Fill in each blank using a word in the box.

business	surfer	respond
waist	collapse	skid

1. The _____ went down to the beach every day.

2. Bill and Gomez were in the _____ of selling paper.

3. The red belt is too tight for my _____.

3 Write the parts for each word.

1. darkness = _____ + _____

2. weekly = _____ + _____

3. responded = _____ + _____

4. hardest = _____ + _____

Errors

Lesson
8

1

1. What was Shirley's plan? _____

2. What were Bert and Shirley to do in the plan?

   _____

   _____

3. What did they plan to charge money for? _____

4. What does "to get a charge out of something" mean?

   _____

5. What did the surfer want to buy with the money he would get?

   _____

6. How did people find out about the sail shop? _____

7. What does "no fish, no pay" mean? _____

   _____

8. Where will you find the surfer now?

   _____

9. Has Shirley's plan made everybody happy? _____

2 **Fill in each blank using a word in the box.**

convert	reply	responded
probably	business	purchased

1. Because it is cloudy today, it will _____ rain tomorrow.

2. Gino _____ two new pairs of shoes.

3. We tried to _____ our garage into a kitchen.

Copyright © SRA/McGraw-Hill. All rights reserved.

Lesson 8   **13**

1

1. a. Is this a story about something that really happened? _____

   b. How do you know? _____

   _____

2. What did Kurt own? _____

3. Why was the mustard jar on the counter? _____

   _____

4. What did Kurt do to the mustard jar every day? _____

5. Where did the strange-looking woman want to take Kurt?

   _____

6. What did the dancing light do to the mustard jar? _____

7. What did the dancing light do to all the other things it hit?

   _____

8. What happened to Kurt and the strange-looking woman?

   _____

9. How long did it take for the fire fighters to get to the snack bar and put out the fire?

   _____

10. How did the jar feel when the chief touched it?

   _____

2 **Fill in each blank using a word in the box.**

several	inspected	future
unusual	convert	exclaimed

1. She _____ the floor to make sure it was clean.

2. "We're cold and hungry!" she _____.

3. Nina had ten cats and _____ dogs.

3 **Write the parts for each word.**

1. inspected   = _____ + _____

2. appearing   = _____ + _____

3. smoothness = _____ + _____

4. faintest   = _____ + _____

1

1. What did the chief discover in the snack bar?

   _____

2. Who were the people from Washington that came to the fire station?

   _____

3. What did the experts want to find out about the mustard jar?

   _____

   _____

4. Where did the experts take the mustard jar?

   _____

5. What do you think "investigation" means?

   _____

6. What was the first thing the experts did to the jar as part of their investigation?

   _____

7. What happened to the jar when the experts heated it up?

   _____

8. What first happened to the jar when the experts gave it three million volts of electricity?

   _____

   _____

9. Then what did the jar do? Name two things.

   a. _____

   b. _____

2 **Fill in each blank using a word in the box.**

probably	investigation	beaker
expert	device	purchase

1. The scientist invented a _____ to fold his clothes.

2. She poured chemicals from a large glass _____.

3. Lila studied animals until she was an _____ on them.

1

1. Why do you think it took nerve to talk to a mustard jar?

_____

2. What did the jar say when one expert asked, "Can you move?"

_____

3. What first happened when the mustard jar tried to move?

_____

4. What did the mustard jar look like when it tried to change shape into a wall?

_____

5. What happened when the jar was quite flat? _____

6. What did the mustard jar sprout when it tried changing shape the second time?

_____

7. What happened when the experts couldn't stop laughing?

_____

8. One expert skidded on the floor. What did he leave behind?

_____

9. Why did one expert say, "You look fine"?

_____

10. What formed in the glass when the mustard jar smiled?

_____

2 Fill in each blank using a word in the box.

laboratory	crease	observed
unusual	future	sprouting

1. The cat carefully _____ the mouse.

2. The seeds in our garden are _____.

3. The _____ was filled with beakers and devices for experiments.

3 Write the parts for each word.

1. squirting = _____ + _____

2. stationed = _____ + _____

3. flatly = _____ + _____

4. aliveness = _____ + _____

1

1. How tall was the mustard jar? _____

2. What did the experts who were giggling do when the jar looked in their direction?

   _____

3. How did the mustard jar cope with the spy?

   _____

4. Did the mustard jar stop the spy? _____

5. What did one of the experts say to the spy to make him behave?

   _____

   _____

6. Who patted the jar on the shoulder?

   _____

7. What is the shoulder of the mustard jar? _____

   _____

8. What kind of tears did the mustard jar have? _____

9. When will the mustard jar run out of mustard? _____

10. How big was the pile of mustard that the jar squirted out?

   _____

   _____

2 **Fill in each blank using a word in the box.**

observe	unfortunate	hesitated
waddled	sprout	crease

1. The _____ cat fell down the stairs.

2. Clark _____ for a moment on the high diving board.

3. The pig was so fat it _____ when it walked.

1

1. What did the mustard jar want to be? _____

2. What did the jar try to do to show that it could hide very well?

   _____

3. What happened to the spy when she laughed at the mustard jar?

   _____

4. Where did the spy chaser take the mustard jar?

   _____

5. What was the spy chaser's plan for the mustard jar?

   _____

   _____

6. Why didn't the spy chaser want to hit the jar with a hammer?

   _____

   _____

7. Where did the spy chaser hit the mustard jar with the hammer?

   _____

8. What happened to the jar when the spy chaser hit it with the hammer?

   _____

9. Was the mustard jar tough? _____

10. Why do you think the spy chaser didn't look too happy at the end of this story?

    _____

    _____

2 **Fill in each blank using a word in the box.**

flinched	observe	unbelievable
innocent	hesitate	waddle

1. His story was just too _____ to be true.

2. They said that James ate the last cookie, but he was _____.

3. When the doctor stuck the needle in Tina's arm, she _____.

3 **Write the parts for each word.**

1. protected = _____ + _____

2. certainly = _____ + _____

3. directing = _____ + _____

4. gentleness = _____ + _____

Lesson 14

1

1. What did the label on the mustard jar say?

   _____

2. The mustard jar was glad to be a member of the _____.

3. What did the boy want? _____

4. What did the boy get? _____

5. The spies came to the store in a _____.

6. How many agents ran into the store? _____

7. How many spies did the helicopter take with it? _____

8. What happened if the mustard jar shot out mustard fast enough?

   _____

9. How many times did the mustard jar hit the floor when it was starting to fly?

   _____

10. a. Do you think the mustard jar will catch the spies? _____

    b. Explain _____

2 **Fill in each blank using a word in the box.**

helicopter	flinch	label
laboratory	tremendous	innocent

1. The _____ on the shirt tells how to wash it.

2. The mountain had a _____ cliff.

3. Robert flies a big blue _____.

1

1. How well did the mustard jar fly at first?

   _____

   _____

2. What happened to the people watching the chase?

   _____

3. What is a stunt? _____

4. What did the cars do? _____

5. What were the boys and girls doing with the mustard?

   _____

6. Which did the children think was better for sliding, mustard or snow?

   _____

7. Why were the workers shoveling mustard into trucks?

   _____

8. After the chase, why would mustard sales be poor?

   _____

   _____

9. Did the mustard jar get better at following the spies? _____

10. What was the mustard jar doing at the end of the story?

   _____

2 **Fill in each blank using a word in the box.**

situation	outfit	continue
tremendous	stunt	label

1. Roberto's favorite _____ is to hang upside down from his helicopter.

2. The horses will _____ running for hours.

3. The mustard jar went to a clothing store and bought a new _____ to wear.

3 **Write the parts for each word.**

1. straightest = _____ + _____

2. staining = _____ + _____

3. disturbed = _____ + _____

4. sharpness = _____ + _____

1

1. How many people were watching the mustard jar head toward the helicopter?

_____

2. How much mustard landed on the helicopter's blades? _____

3. Where did the helicopter land?

_____

4. What did the helicopter hit in the intersection? _____

5. Why was the police officer's outfit yellow?

_____

6. What happened when many people phoned the Secret Agents?

_____

7. Why were the people complaining?

_____

8. Why did the chief want to get rid of the mustard jar?

_____

_____

9. Why was the mustard jar proud?

_____

10. What did the mustard jar call itself?

_____

2 **Fill in each blank using a word in the box.**

| outfit | collided | instant |
| deceptive | intersection | situation |

1. When the experts lied to the mustard jar, they were being _____.

2. Anna bruised her knee when she _____ with the bicycle.

3. The two cars collided at the _____.

1 **Copy the sentence that tells the main idea of the story.**

1. Both Doris and Jane were teachers, and both took scuba diving lessons.

2. Jane and Doris rented a boat when they arrived at Key West.

3. When Jane and Doris took their first dive, Jane was a little afraid.

4. Jane and Doris decided to go to the Florida Keys on vacation and dive for sunken treasure.

_____

_____

2 1. What kind of work did Jane do? _____

2. How did Jane injure her leg? _____

3. What did Jane want to do on her vacation? _____

4. What kind of maps had the two women studied?

_____

_____

5. What kind of classes had Doris and Jane taken? _____

6. How long was the old boat that Doris and Jane rented? _____

7. How long was Jane underwater before her ears stopped hurting? _____

8. What color did Doris's suit look underwater? _____

9. What is a school of fish? _____

3 **Fill in each blank using a word in the box.**

buoy	occasional	tremendous
label	gymnastics	gear

1. The _____ marked an underwater reef.

2. Bill's favorite sport is _____.

3. Jane needed the right diving _____ before she could dive.

1

1. How did Doris get weather information?

   _____

2. When did the Coast Guard expect a northeast wind to move in?

   _____

3. Where were Jane and Doris going? _____

4. Why was the coral reef dangerous? _____

5. What gear was tied down in front of the boat? _____

6. Name two other things the women took with them in the boat.

   _____

   _____

7. How was the reef marked? _____

8. How could Jane and Doris get stranded? _____

9. What did the coral reef look like? _____

   _____

10. How do you think Jane felt as she looked down at the coral reef?

   _____

2 **Fill in each blank using a word in the box.**

pressure	reply	glimpse
prop	stranded	beaker

1. The boat's _____ broke on the reef.

2. The old man had been _____ on the island for forty years.

3. The water _____ hurt Sam's ears when he was down fifty feet.

Errors

1

1. How long ago had the ship gone down?

_____

2. What is a reef made of? _____

3. Why was it hard to say just where the ship went down?

_____

4. How long did Doris and Jane plan to stay underwater? _____

5. Did Jane seem to have trouble swimming with a leg brace? _____

6. What kind of watches did Jane and Doris have? _____

7. What kind of markers did the watches have? _____

_____

8. Why is it dangerous to get too close to a reef?

_____

9. What does the movement of underwater plants indicate?

_____

10. What did the women find attached to the reef? _____

11. How much was each sponge worth? _____

2 Fill in each blank using a word in the box.

current	nitrogen	glimpse
location	unsteady	indicate

1. No one could find the _____ of the hidden treasure.

2. The skater fell down because he was _____.

3. Jane and Doris set up buoys to _____ that divers were in the water.

3 Write the parts for each word.

1. meaning = _____ + _____

2. screeching = _____ + _____

3. steepness = _____ + _____

4. roughly = _____ + _____

Errors

1

1. Why did Jane let go of the coral? _____

_____

2. Why was Jane going with the current?

_____

3. Why did Jane have to squint to see the dark form below?

_____

_____

4. Where was the ship? _____

5. How did Jane feel when she saw the ship? _____

6. Jane's heart was beating like the _____

_____.

7. What did Jane feel forming on her arms? _____

8. If a diver comes up too fast, the diver can get _____.

9. What can nitrogen bubbles do to a diver?

_____

10. Why did Jane want to get up to the surface? _____

_____

2 **Fill in each blank using a word in the box.**

indicate	surface	nitrogen
creature	ledge	sunken

1. Jane swam up to the _____ of the water.

2. She swam up slowly so that no _____ bubbles would form in her blood.

3. The mountain climber stood on a narrow _____ 500 feet above the ground.

Errors

1. How did Jane feel when she saw the ship? _____

2. How far was the ship from the reef? _____

3. Why did Jane ask to rest before going back with Doris to see the ship? _____

   _____

4. What was Jane's plan for going back to see the ship with Doris?

   _____

   _____

5. Why couldn't Jane and Doris go below sixty feet?

   _____

6. How did Jane know they were in the wrong place? (Name two reasons.)

   a. _____

   b. _____

7. Jane suddenly realized she had gone too deep. How did she know? _____

   _____

8. Jane knew she should not dive below sixty feet. Why did she stop looking at her depth

   gauge and go too far? _____

   _____

   _____

9. Why couldn't Jane go to the surface immediately?

   _____

10. Why do you think Doris had been signaling Jane?

   _____

   _____

2 **Fill in each blank using a word in the box.**

| nitrogen | decide | fierce |
| realized | sprawled | immediately |

1. The sleepy cat _____ across the bed.

2. The _____ tiger roared and snarled.

3. After Josie and Carla packed quickly, they left _____ for Hawaii.

3 **Write the parts for each word.**

1. remaining = _____ + _____

2. warmest = _____ + _____

3. interested = _____ + _____

4. darkness = _____ + _____

1. 1. Doris couldn't understand Jane when she said, "I'm running out of air." So how did Doris know what to do? _____

_____

2. What did Jane do when she got the new air tank? _____

_____

_____

3. Why did Jane want to string some spare tanks on the anchor line?

_____

4. Why wouldn't the woman rent Jane and Doris a boat one day?

_____

5. Why were Jane and Doris nervous about not diving once the weather turned bad?

_____

_____

6. Here are some things Jane and Doris did on their "wasted" day.

Number them 1, 2, 3, 4, 5, and 6 to show the order in which they happened.

_____ They watched television.

_____ They walked along the beach again.

_____ They went to bed.

_____ They ate seafood.

_____ They walked along the beach in the morning.

_____ They drove to a seafood stand.

7. How long did Jane and Doris kill time? _____

8. On the third day why did Jane want to get to the reef really fast? _____

_____

9. How much danger do you think that Jane and Doris are in at the end of the story?

_____

10. a. If the woman at the dock had given you the same advice she gave Jane and Doris,

would you have gone out to look for the ship? _____

b. Why? _____

_____

2 | **Fill in each blank using a word in the box.**

pleaded	sprawling	gasping
exclaimed	advice	nervous

1. The runner lay on the ground _____ for breath.

2. Carlos _____ with his parents to take him to the circus.

3. The scary movie made Melinda _____ and jumpy.

Copy the sentence that tells the main idea of the story.

1. The sky was gray and became very dark later in the day.

2. The women anchored their boat in the same spot they had before and dove from that spot.

3. Jane became frightened after she found a sunken ship where a skull seemed to be staring at her.

4. The divers carried spare air tanks so they would be able to stay under water longer.

_____

_____

1. Where did Jane and Doris put the air tank?

_____

2. Which route did Jane and Doris take to reach the ship? _____

_____

3. Just as Jane and Doris were ready to begin to dive, something could have changed their minds. What was it?

_____

4. What pulled Jane and Doris through the water? _____

5. If you were diving very deep like Jane, how do you think your body would feel? Name two things. _____

_____

6. How did the ship look to Jane as she got close to it?

_____

7. What was the ship's rail covered with? _____

8. What was the deck covered with? _____

9. Why didn't Jane want to go back down to the ship?

_____

10. When Jane was fifty feet from the surface she could no longer see the ship. Why?

Underline the best answer.

Jane's mask was cloudy, so the sky looked dark.

It was late, and the sun was going down.

Storm clouds made the sky very dark.

3 **Fill in each blank using a word in the box.**

announced	investigation	wispy
gymnastics	suspended	anchor

1. Bill's father _____ that the family was moving to New York.

2. The _____ stopped the boat from floating away.

3. The punching bag was _____ from the ceiling by a rope.

4 **Write the parts for each word.**

1. brightest = _____ + _____

2. freshly = _____ + _____

3. sheltered = _____ + _____

4. modeling = _____ + _____

Errors

1

1. Why did Jane and Doris need protection from the storm?

   _____

2. What did Jane and Doris see to protect the boat? _____

3. What happened to the boat when the waves rolled over the low places along the reef?

   _____

4. Describe what the water looked and sounded like during the storm.

   _____

   _____

   _____

5. How long did the wind blow? _____

6. a. When the wind stopped blowing, was the storm over? _____

   b. How do you know?

   _____

7. Why was it hard for Jane and Doris to talk as the wind blew?

   _____

8. What does "venture" mean? _____

   _____

9. Why would Jane and Doris remember that day for a long time?

   _____

10. a. Do you think Jane and Doris will go back to the ship after what happened to them?

    _____

    b. Why? _____

    _____

2 **Fill in each blank using a word in the box.**

glanced	unsteady	protection
suggests	location	plead

1. The rabbit _____ back to see if the dogs were still chasing him.

2. The woman's umbrella gave her some _____ from the rainstorm.

3. A quiet house _____ to me that no one is home.

Copy the sentence that tells the main idea of the story.

1. Jane refused to go back inside the ship again.

2. The women rented a speedboat because they wanted to return to the sunken ship quickly.

3. The women made a deal to split all the profits with the salvage company.

4. Jane and Doris returned to the dive site and claimed the sunken ship as salvage.

_____

_____

2 1. Why didn't Jane want to go back to the ship? List two reasons.

a. _____

_____

b. _____

_____

2. In Item 1, one of your answers should tell what frightened Jane the most. **Circle** that answer.

3. What kind of flag did Jane and Doris put up along with the diving flags?

_____

4. What color was this new flag? _____

5. Why did Jane and Doris want to put up this flag? _____

_____

_____

6. What kind of deal did Jane and Doris make with the salvage company?

_____

_____

7. What kind of gear did Mike wear? _____

Copyright © SRA/McGraw-Hill. All rights reserved.

8. Name three kinds of treasures that were on the boat. _____

_____

_____

9. a. Do you think the ship was a pirate ship? _____

b. Why? _____

_____

_____

10. Why do you think Jane was happy with her trip?

_____

_____

_____

3 **Fill in each blank using a word in the box.**

decide	prop	statue
marine	salvage	figurehead

1. Many _____ creatures were washed up on the beach.

2. Jane brought up bottles and old instruments, but there was no gold in the

_____.

3. On the front of the ship was a _____.

Errors

1

1. How does a redwood tree's life begin? _____

2. How big is a redwood cone? _____

3. How big are redwood seeds? _____

_____

4. Which kind of trees have the thickest trunks? _____

5. How would you describe a giant sequoia trunk to show how thick it is?

_____

_____

6. How tall is a very tall redwood?

_____

7. Which trees are the tallest in the world? _____

8. When did the seeds from the redwood tree flutter from the cone?

_____

9. Why didn't the seeds fall from the cone when it was raining?

_____

_____

10. How many seeds survived? _____

2 Fill in each blank using a word in the box.

tunnel	snaked	fluttered
salvage	drizzly	emerged

1. The baby birds _____ their wings.

2. The door opened, and a tall man _____.

3. The road _____ around the mountains instead of tunneling through them.

3 Write the parts for each word.

1. untended = _____ + _____ + _____

2. explaining = _____ + _____ + _____

3. excitement = _____ + _____ + _____

4. uninteresting = _____ + _____ + _____

Errors

1. 1. How many pounds of seed did the parent tree produce?

   _____

   2. How many seeds survived beyond the first year? _____

   3. Why was our redwood seed lucky? _____

   _____

   4. **Put a check next to the correct answers.**

   Our redwood seed was fortunate because—

   _____ a. it landed in a place that was very dry.

   _____ b. it landed near piles of fresh brown dirt.

   _____ c. it landed in a place that would receive sunlight.

   _____ d. it landed on a part of the forest floor covered with litter.

   _____ e. it spent the winter lodged in a crack between two mounds of dirt.

   5. What happened so our seed could receive sunlight?

   _____

   _____

   6. What kind of light can redwoods survive in?

   _____

   7. What kind of light do redwoods not grow well in? _____

   8. Where did our seed become lodged?

   _____

   9. What does "lodged" mean? _____

   10. When would the seed be ready to grow?

   _____

2 **Fill in each blank using a word in the box.**

severe	mole	ledge
nervous	slime	location

1. She fell into the muddy pool and emerged covered with _____.

2. The _____ lived in a hole in the ground.

3. Everyone found some protection from the _____ storm.

1

1. What are baby trees called? _____

2. How high did our seedling grow during its first summer?

_____

3. Why did our seedling receive sunlight? _____

_____

4. What is a sapling? _____

5. How tall was the sapling after six years? _____

6. Before the fire, how much was the sapling ready to grow?

_____

7. How did the fire begin? _____

8. Which trees did the fire burn to the ground?

_____

9. What did the sapling look like after the fire swept through the forest?

_____

_____

10. **Draw a line from each of the items in the left column to the correct item in the right column.**

    a. the sapling   • less than an inch

    b. seedling after first summer   • over 400 feet

    c. the parent tree   • a half inch

    d. seedling gets two leaves   • twelve feet

    e. seedling straightens up   • three inches

2 **Fill in each blank using a word in the box.**

charred	swells	announced
smoldering	breaker	torch

1. The fire seemed to be out, but inside, parts of the logs were still _____.

2. The logs had been _____ black by the fire.

3. Rico took a _____ into the cave to light his way.

1

1. Why didn't anyone put the fire out? _____

2. **Fill in the blanks:**

   After the flames died down, bigger trees _____ for

   _____. When it _____ in

   late fall, the _____ died out.

3. How many shoots did the roots of the young redwood send up? _____

4. Why can't a fire kill a young redwood?

   _____

5. How tall was the sapling six years after the fire?

   _____

6. What does a burl look like? _____

7. Why do the lower branches on a redwood die?

   _____

8. How tall was the redwood after eighty years?

   _____

9. How big was the base of the trunk after eighty years?

   _____

10. Read each item. Circle **True** if you think the item is correct. Circle **False** if you think
    the item is not correct.

    a. The fire happened more than two thousand years ago.   True   False

    b. The trees began to grow again in the fall after the fire took place.   True   False

    c. Redwood saplings have no natural enemy.   True   False

    d. The roots of the charred redwood were dead.   True   False

2 **Fill in each blank using a word in the box.**

collided	toppled	frequent
ignited	suggest	original

1. The unsteady vase _____ over.

2. The truck and taxicab _____ at the intersection.

3. Your _____ home is the very first one you have.

3 **Write the parts for each word.**

1. uncloaked = _____ + _____ + _____

2. secondly = _____ + _____

3. uncertainly = _____ + _____ + _____

4. extended = _____ + _____ + _____

Errors

1

1. How old was our redwood tree when it became a good seed producer?

   _____

2. How long would our redwood continue to produce seeds?

   _____

3. What happens to the rate of growth of the redwood when it becomes a mature tree?

   _____

4. Where did the fire begin? _____

   _____

5. Which trees did the fire touch first? _____

6. How long did the fire smolder? _____

7. After the fire, what did the remaining trees look like?

   _____

8. What part of the tree trunk is the living part?

   _____

9. Why did the mature redwoods survive the fire?

   _____

10. Why did the oaks and sugar pines die in the fire?

   _____

2 **Fill in each blank using a word in the box.**

| mature | snaked | wispy |
| deafening | leveled | original |

1. The wind blew with a _____ roar.

2. When the caterpillar becomes _____, it will be a butterfly.

3. After the forest was _____, there were only a few tree stumps left.

1

1. Which trees adapt best to new situations, young trees or old trees?

_____

2. What might happen to a mature tree if a tree next to it is cut down?

_____

3. How old was the redwood when the fire burned every needle from it?

_____

4. How old was the redwood when it lost its top in a storm?

_____

5. How long did it take for the redwood to grow its top back?

_____

6. Why did the redwood have a hole in its base?

_____

7. What animals used the hole in the base of our redwood most?

_____

8. How big was the hole in the base of our redwood?

_____

9. Even if they are exposed to the rain, boards made from redwood don't _____.

2 **Fill in each blank using a word in the box.**

toppled	installed	litter
adapted	canopy	sprouts

1. The picnic table had a _____ over it to protect it from the rain.

2. The tree was cut down, but it sent up new _____.

3. Nita _____ to the cold by wearing more clothing.

Errors

1

1. What's the most remarkable thing about the wood from the redwoods?

   _____

2. Name two faults of redwoods. _____

   _____

3. What's dangerous about a mature redwood that's not surrounded by other trees?

   _____

   _____

4. a. What is the name of the park in which our tree lives?

   _____

   b. How big is that park? _____

   c. In what year was the park formed? _____

2

Fill in each blank using a word in the box.

outskirts	charred	original
polite	nature	drizzly

1. They chose to live on the _____ of town, where they could raise chickens.

2. The outside of the house was badly _____ by the fire.

3. He said "thank you" so often that we thought he was just too _____.

3

Write the parts for each word.

1. replace = _____ + _____

2. unclearly = _____ + _____ + _____

3. exclaiming = _____ + _____ + _____

4. unloaded = _____ + _____ + _____

1

1. What kind of job did Bruce have?

   _____

2. Why did Bruce work through the lunch hour?

   _____

3. What did Bruce usually do first—go for a walk, park his car in the garage, or eat dinner?

   _____

4. How did Bruce feel about his neighbors?

   _____

5. Why didn't Bruce like lights?_____

6. What would Bruce do after dinner? _____

7. Why did Bruce have trouble hearing the birds?

   _____

8. What did Bruce hear while lying in bed?

   _____

9. Describe the place Bruce wished for. _____

   _____

10. Where was Bruce when he woke up? _____

2 **Fill in each blank using a word in the box.**

| insurance | freeway | bothersome |
| sprouts | torch | mature |

1. The _____ bugs swarmed around her head all night.

2. Joe got in his new car and raced down the _____.

3. After their house burned down, the people received money from their

   _____ company.

3

Copy the sentence that tells the main idea of the story.

1. Bruce worked hard as vice president of an insurance company but didn't talk much to his neighbors.

2. Every night, Bruce wished for a simple life, and one morning he woke up on a peaceful beach.

3. Every day, Bruce had sore eyes and a pain in his head after he came home from work.

4. Bruce lived alone and realized that he was a grouch.

_____

_____

_____

1

1. How did Bruce know the water was ocean water? _____

2. By the evening of the second day, did Bruce think he was still dreaming? _____

3. What did Bruce prove by walking all the way around the island?

   _____

4. What did Bruce eat?

   _____

5. What did Bruce drink? _____

6. Where did the fresh water come from? _____

7. How did Bruce feel by the end of the third day on the island?

   _____

8. What did Bruce wish for on the fourth day on the island?

   _____

9. In what ways did Bruce show he was happy to have other people on the island?

   a. _____

   b. _____

   _____

10. When he discovered there was no water, what did Bruce suggest they drink?

   _____

2   **Fill in each blank using a word in the box.**

deserve	adapted	statue
breadfruit	mole	canopy

1. I mowed Mr. Lewis's lawn, and I _____ to be paid for it.

2. José's favorite cooked fruit is _____.

3. Angela _____ to the heat by taking it easy.

1

1. Name two things you need to stay alive. _____

2. How long could Bruce live without water? _____

3. How long could he live without food? _____

4. Which problem is more immediate, the food problem or the water problem?

_____

5. Bruce said, "We can solve this problem if _____."

6. Name two things you could do to get water if you were on Bruce's island.

   a. _____

   b. _____

7. Why did Bruce suggest making digging tools on the fourth day?

_____

8. Why did Bruce decide to dig for water rather than boil seawater?

_____

9. Where did Bruce and the others go to dig for water?

_____

10. How did Bruce make a digging tool? _____

_____

11. How deep was the hole when signs of moisture began to appear?

_____

2 Fill in each blank using a word in the box.

bored	brittle	shattering
disturbed	charred	deserved

1. The mother cat was very _____ when she couldn't find one of her kittens.

2. Marie had nothing to do. She was very _____.

3. Jerry _____ better pay for his hard work.

3 Write the parts for each word.

1. undisturbed = _____ + _____ + _____

2. reporter = _____ + _____ + _____

3. remodeling = _____ + _____ + _____

4. unequally = _____ + _____ + _____

1 1. Why did Bruce solve the water problem first? _____

_____

2. Did the people have to find water to survive? _____

3. What were the first two tools Bruce made to solve the food problem?

_____

4. What did he use to make these tools?

_____

5. Were Bruce and the others able to get a lot of food by hunting? _____

6. When the hunt was over, what had the hunters killed?

_____

7. What did the hunters spend most of their time doing? _____

_____

8. Why did Bruce make a fire? _____

9. Did the people have to find food to survive? _____

10. How many fish did the people catch the first time they threw out the net? _____

11. What was Bruce tired of listening to? _____

12. Why do you think Bruce might have been surprised to hear the woman talk?

_____

2 **Fill in each blank using a word in the box.**

shortage	investigation	brittle
fluttered	flexible	waddled

1. The children twisted _____ hangers into different shapes.

2. When the wind blew, leaves _____ to the ground.

3. The classes had to share books because there was a _____ of them.

Errors

1

1. Name the four things that a person needs to stay alive.

   _____

2. Why did Bruce solve the water problem before he solved the food problem?

   _____

3. What was the weather like? _____

4. What did Centa fear would happen if they couldn't find a way to stay warm?

   _____

5. What did Bruce and the others do first to solve the cold problem?

   _____

6. What did they do next to stay warm? _____

7. What is a shelter? _____

8. Why didn't Bruce want a big fire in the shelter?

   _____

9. What did Bruce suggest they use to make warm clothes?

   _____

10. What was the problem with using rabbit hides and bird feathers to make warm clothes?

    _____

    _____

2 **Fill in each blank using a word in the box.**

site	insurance	disturbed
tingly	flexible	suitable

1. The bear hit the beehive and _____ the bees.

2. The meadow was a nice _____ for a picnic.

3. His fingers felt cold and _____.

1

1. If you had both a water problem and a food problem, which would you solve first?

   _____

2. Of which would you die first, a lack of air or of water?

   _____

3. If you had both an air problem and a water problem, which would you solve first?

   _____

4. If you had both a food problem and an air problem, which would you solve first?

   _____

5. If you had more than one life problem at the same time, which would you solve first?

   _____

6. Name three things that Bruce and the others did to solve the warmth problem.

   a. _____

   b. _____

   c. _____

7. What tool did Centa make for sewing clothes? _____

8. What did Bruce use for thread? _____

9. Name two types of material that Bruce planned to use for making clothes.

   _____

10. How many baby pigs were with the mother pig? _____

11. What did Bruce and the others use to carry the pig? _____

2 **Fill in each blank using a word in the box.**

hoist	site	chore
breadfruit	provide	commented

1. "What unusually warm weather this is!" the man _____.

2. She tried to _____ the heavy weight.

3. Tony's _____ was washing dishes every day.

3 **Write the parts for each word.**

1. unsheltered = _____ + _____ + _____

2. remarked = _____ + _____ + _____

3. reconstruct = _____ + _____

4. discover = _____ + _____

1

1. Why was the new net better than the net the people had made before?

   _____

2. What did the people build to catch crabs? _____

   _____

3. What did the people use for bowls? _____

4. What did the people use for spoons? _____

5. Write **life** in front of each life problem and **comfort** in front of each comfort problem.

   a. _____ You have no protection against zero-degree weather.

   b. _____ There's a small hole in the roof.

   c. _____ You have no water.

   d. _____ There is no food.

   e. _____ You have to eat bananas every day.

   f. _____ You have no friends.

   g. _____ You have to walk four miles to get water.

   h. _____ There is no air.

6. The people had a plan for working around the shelter. Did each person do all the

   different jobs there were to do? _____

7. Name two jobs that had to be done after Bruce and the others came back with the
   young pigs.

   a. _____

   b. _____

8. What were the baby pigs given to eat? _____

2 **Fill in each blank using a word in the box.**

chimney	hoist	chowder
examined	deserve	procedure

1. They had fish _____ for lunch.

2. Smoke came out of the _____.

3. He _____ his newspaper closely.

1   **1.** Write **life** in front of each life problem and **comfort** in front of each comfort problem.

a. _____ There is lots of food on the island, but none of it tastes good.

b. _____ There is no food on the island, and there are no animals in the sea.

c. _____ There are six people, and there is enough food on the island

and in the sea to keep two people alive.

d. _____ There's a small hole in the roof.

e. _____ You have to walk three miles to get water.

f. _____ You have no water.

2. Did everybody on the island have a specific job? _____

3. Who was now in charge of making clothes for the people?

_____

4. Name the animals they now had.

_____

5. Name three jobs the woman in charge of the animals had to do.

_____

_____

_____

6. How did Bruce know that the trees were dead?

_____

7. Why would some animals die if the trees died?

_____

8. How could Bruce and the others get food if all the trees died?

_____

9. When must people move from one place to another?

_____

_____

2 **Fill in each blank using a word in the box.**

extension	argument	deadlocked
solved	chore	remodel

1. He added an _____ to the end of his fishing pole.

2. The women had an _____ about who owned the goat.

3. Neither side could win the fight. The sides were _____.

1

1. What was the first argument about? _____

_____

2. Why didn't Bruce have a lot of faith in planting seeds?

_____

_____

_____

3. The people were in a deadlock. What does "deadlock" mean?

_____

_____

4. Circle the numbers that could lead to a deadlock.

4   5   6   7   8   9   10   11   12   13   14   15   16

5. Why didn't some people want Centa to have two votes?

_____

_____

6. What was the rule about the stone?

_____

_____

7. Whose side won?

_____

8. What was the first law made on the island?

_____

9. What was the rule about individuals doing what they wanted?

_____

_____

10. Would it have been all right for individuals to change the agreement if more than half

the people decided not to follow it?_____

2 **Fill in each blank using a word in the box.**

decision	solution	examine
husks	verses	argument

1. After the argument, Toshi made a _____ to move to California.

2. They found a _____ to their problem.

3. Sam lost the _____ with Cindy.

3 **Write the parts for each word.**

1. explained = _____ + _____ + _____

2. distracted = _____ + _____ + _____

3. extend = _____ + _____

4. remounted = _____ + _____ + _____

1

1. How much gold did Bruce and the others want for the fish they had? _____

2. What did Bruce and the others pay for every five bananas? _____

3. Why did they want to trade for bananas?

   _____

4. How much would a boatful of bananas have been worth if Bruce's island had had lots

   of healthy banana trees? _____

5. Can you make up a rule about how much things are worth? Think about what makes

   the price of bananas go up and down. _____

   _____

   _____

6. To be able to trade four hundred fish for two thousand bananas, the people had to

   solve some problems. List two problems. _____

   _____

   _____

   _____

7. How did the people try to solve the two problems you listed in item 6?

   _____

   _____

   _____

   _____

8. How did the people avoid a deadlock on whether they should build a barge?

   _____

9. a. Do you think this is a fair way to get out of a deadlock? _____

b. Why?_____

_____

10. Why did the people need to build a barge?

_____

_____

2 Fill in each blank using a word in the box.

enforces	barge	suitable
prevent	deadlocked	solution

1. The teacher _____ the rules.

2. He held on to his dog to _____ it from running away.

3. The _____ carried garbage down the river.

3 Copy the sentence that tells the main idea of the story.

1. The people decided to trade fish with people from an island that had lots of bananas.

2. The people on the island were not successful at raising crops.

3. The people decided not to steal the bananas from the people who came to their island.

4. One of the people on the island got two votes so there would not be a deadlock.

_____

_____

1

1. Tell at least three things about the barge.

_____

_____

_____

2. What is a school of fish? _____

3. What did Bruce and Jonas use for bait? _____

4. What kinds of fish did they catch? _____

5. How many fish did Bruce and Jonas catch? _____

6. Bruce and Jonas caught a large, blue tuna fish. How much did it weigh?

_____

7. At what point did Jonas realize that some fish should be worth more than five bananas?

_____

8. How much were most of the fish worth?

_____

9. If Bruce hadn't shown the woman the minnows, how much would she have said the big

fish was worth? _____

10. Bruce made up a rule about what was worth five bananas. What rule did he make up?

_____

11. Was the woman displeased about the deal? _____

2 **Fill in each blank using a word in the box.**

enforced	remarked	decision
advice	evaporated	pressure

1. All the water _____ from the pot.

2. "What lovely flowers," she _____ .

3. The prisoner made a _____ to escape.

1

1. Name three things that the people on the island had to do to prepare smoked fish.

   _____

   _____

   _____

   _____

2. Why did the people go to the trouble of making smoked fish?

   _____

   _____

3. What would happen to the price of fish if fish jumped out of the water and onto the beach?

   _____

4. What would happen to the price of fish if the people had to work five hours to catch

   each fish?_____

5. Make up a rule about the price of fish and the amount of work it takes to catch fish.

   _____

   _____

   _____

6. What did Bruce and Centa do to get the woman to trade for smoked fish?

   _____

7. Bruce didn't really believe that the smoked fish were worth nine bananas each. Why did he set the price at nine bananas when he began bargaining with the woman?

   _____

   _____

8. What did Bruce and the woman agree would be a fair price for smoked fish?

_____

9. Why would the price of smoked fish be higher than the price of fresh fish?

_____

10. What do you think would have happened if the woman had not liked the taste of smoked fish?

_____

_____

11. Why wasn't there a demand for fish on Bruce's island?

_____

12. Why was there a demand for bananas on Bruce's island?

_____

13. If the demand for something goes up, what will the price do? _____

2 **Fill in each blank using a word in the box.**

demand	prevented	minnows
barge	disapproved	remarked

1. There was a much greater _____ for ice during the summer.

2. He _____ of violence.

3. Abby _____ a forest fire by putting out her camp fire.

3 **Write the parts for each word.**

1. disappear = _____ + _____

2. unscratched = _____ + _____ + _____

Lesson 44 **77**

1

1. Is a need for insurance a life problem or a comfort problem?

   _____

2. Write **survival** in front of each survival problem and **comfort** in front of each comfort problem.

   a. _____ You have to eat bananas and fish every day.

   b. _____ There is no air.

   c. _____ You have to walk two miles for food.

   d. _____ You have no friends around.

   e. _____ You have only summer clothes to wear in zero-degree weather.

3. Why do you think Bruce wants to go back to the city?

   _____

4. What day did Bruce return to his home in the suburb?

   _____

5. What made Bruce think that his trip to the island was not a dream?

   _____

6. What was Bruce's motto?

   _____

   _____

   _____

7. If there was only a little demand for insurance, would the price of insurance be high

   or low? _____

8. Did Bruce need a car to stay alive? _____

9. Let's say Bruce dreams himself into another situation and has all these problems at the same time:

a. _____ It is very cold sometimes.   c. _____ There is no food.

b. _____ There is no air.   d. _____ There is no water.

List the order in which Bruce should solve these problems.
Put a number (1, 2, 3, or 4) in front of each of these problems.

2 **Fill in each blank using a word in the box.**

exceptionally	evaporated	immediately
deceptive	examined	enforced

1. The young flute player was _____ talented.

2. All the water in the pan on the stove had _____.

3. The police strictly _____ the parking rules.

3 **Copy the sentence that tells the main idea of the story.**

1. Bruce woke up one morning, heard the hum of the air conditioner, and realized that he was back in his home.

2. On Bruce's dresser was the ax that he had made from a tree branch on the island.

3. Island life had changed Bruce and the way he thought about work, other people, and his life.

4. Bruce realized that he worked fifteen hours a day on the island, but he was happy doing that work.

_____

_____

_____

1

1. Describe the great plain.

   _____

   _____

2. What kind of animals lived on the plain?

   _____

3. What predators lived on the plain? _____

4. How hot was it on the plain?

   _____

5. How many horns did the triceratops have? _____

6. What animal living today looks something like a triceratops? _____

7. How much would a full-grown triceratops weigh? _____

8. A triceratops would weigh as much as _____ elephants.

9. How tall would a triceratops be? _____

10. How much did a triceratops eat each day?

    _____

    _____

2 Fill in each blank using a word in the box.

protested	grazing	reptile
mammals	thrashed	herd

1. There was a large _____ of cows in the field.

2. The cows were _____ on sweet green grass.

3. Like the snake, the triceratops was a _____.

1 1. What did Tekla already know how to do when she was born?

_____

2. What kind of animal was the triceratops, a grazing animal or a predator?

_____

3. What two senses are well developed in most grazing animals?

_____

4. a. Where does a predator have eyes?

_____

   b. Why? _____

_____

5. a. Where does a grazing animal have eyes?

_____

   b. Why? _____

6. What kind of animal was the ornithomimid, a grazing animal or a predator?

_____

7. What did the ornithomimid look like?

_____

_____

8. What did an ornithomimid like to eat? _____

9. For how long had the brontosaurs been extinct when Tekla was born?

_____

2 Fill in each blank using a word in the box.

foul-tasting	taut	programmed
roamed	keen	reptiles

1. The pack of wolves _____ through the forest.

2. The wolves' sense of smell was very _____.

3. The rotten cheese was _____.

3 Copy the sentence that tells the main idea of the story.

1. Tekla was a grazing animal that had a keen sense of smell and sharp vision.

2. The triceratops eggs were buried in the sand near the edge of a cliff.

3. The animal that ate the triceratops eggs looked like a large ostrich with a lizard tail and very sharp teeth.

4. Tekla was the only baby triceratops in her family that escaped the attack of an ornithomimid.

_____

_____

_____

4 Write the parts for each word.

1. previewed = _____ + _____ + _____

2. unlikely = _____ + _____ + _____

3. pretender = _____ + _____ + _____

4. disgusting = _____ + _____ + _____

1

1. What do grazing animals eat? _____

2. What do predators eat? _____

3. Write **grazing animal** or **predator** in front of each animal.

   _____ a. triceratops

   _____ b. lion

   _____ c. tyrannosaur

4. How were the ornithomimid and the tyrannosaur alike?

   _____

   _____

5. How tall was the tyrannosaur?

   _____

6. Why did the tyrannosaur look strange? _____

   _____

7. What attracted the predators?

   _____

8. Why were few ornithomimid bones left the next morning?

   _____

9. Describe the grazing habits of the triceratops. _____

   _____

10. How did Tekla react when the snake struck at her?

   _____

2 **Fill in each blank using a word in the box.**

leisurely	aroused	feasting
scavengers	ignored	programmed

1. Mark _____ his dog's whines.

2. The _____ chewed the bones that the lions left behind.

3. The snail went at a _____ pace.

1

1. Name five insects that lived on the plain.

_____

_____

2. Name two trees living on the plain that are alive today.

_____

3. For how long did dinosaurs live on the earth?

_____

4. What is the name of the last time period when dinosaurs lived?

_____

5. How long after dinosaurs became extinct did humans inhabit the earth?

_____

6. Compare how the young triceratops behaved at the water hole with how the adults behaved.

_____

_____

_____

7. What do carnivores eat? _____

8. What do herbivores eat? _____

9. Is a grazing animal a carnivore or a herbivore? _____

10. Is a predator a carnivore or a herbivore? _____

2 **Fill in each blank using a word in the box.**

foliage	pranced	resumed
unison	slither	scramble

1. They read the poem in _____.

2. The colts _____ across the field.

3. Billy _____ cooking after he got off the phone.

Errors

1

1. Why did the crocodile let go of Tekla?

_____

_____

2. How does pain serve intelligent animals?

_____

3. What animal probably reacts most to pain? _____

4. How did the size of the brain of a triceratops compare with the size of its body?

_____

5. Name three things the instincts of a triceratops told it to do.

_____

_____

_____

6. Describe the climate of the place where the dinosaurs lived.

_____

7. Write **carnivore** or **herbivore** in front of each animal.

_____ a. lion

_____ b. triceratops

_____ c. cow

_____ d. tyrannosaur

8. How long after the dinosaurs became extinct did humans inhabit the earth?

_____

9. Name the two trees living on the plain that are alive today.

_____

2 Fill in each blank using a word in the box.

alert	visible	secluded
daggerlike	gash	unison

1. The tiger smiled, showing her _____ teeth.

2. She couldn't find her purse even though it was plainly _____.

3. The thorn left a nasty _____ in her arm.

3 Copy the sentence that tells the main idea of the story.

1. Tekla weighed over 4,000 pounds but was far from being full-grown.

2. Tekla managed to survive her first year of life.

3. A crocodile attacked Tekla but did not injure her badly.

4. A female triceratops who wanted to lay eggs chased Tekla away.

_____

_____

4 Write the parts for each word.

1. tricycle = _____ + _____

2. unarmed = _____ + _____ + _____

3. extending = _____ + _____ + _____

4. prehistoric = _____ + _____

1

1. How would six triceratops do in a battle with one tyrannosaur?

   _____

2. How much would a full-grown triceratops weigh? _____

3. In what two ways did Tekla behave differently when she became an adult?

   a. _____

   b. _____

4. How old was Tekla when she had her first battle with a tyrannosaur?

   _____

5. Why did a triceratops always try to face the predator?

   _____

6. What two senses are well developed in most grazing animals?

   _____

7. What is the name of the last time period in which dinosaurs lived?

   _____

8. What do carnivores eat? _____

9. What do herbivores eat? _____

10. For how long did dinosaurs inhabit the earth? _____

2

Fill in each blank using a word in the box.

faked	secluded	viciously
vegetation	alert	knee-deep

1. Lena stood _____ in the mud.

2. The big lion snarled _____.

3. The _____ was thick on the hills.

1

1. How were a dinosaur's back legs different from its front legs? _____

_____

2. The tyrannosaur jumped around like _____.

3. How did Tekla get away from the tyrannosaur? _____

_____

_____

4. How did many dinosaurs act after the battle?

_____

5. Why didn't Tekla remember her battle with the tyrannosaur?

_____

_____

6. When the battle was over, Tekla knew only that she should _____.

7. Name two trees living on the plain that are alive today.

_____

8. How long after the dinosaurs became extinct did humans inhabit the earth?

_____

9. Write **grazing animal** or **predator** in front of each animal.

_____ a. tyrannosaur

_____ b. triceratops

_____ c. horse

_____ d. lion

10. What did the ornithomimid like to eat? _____

2 **Fill in each blank using a word in the box.**

faked	ribs	trampled
shrill	submerge	visible

1. The horses _____ the vegetation.

2. The bird song was high and _____.

3. Your _____ are in your chest.

3 **Copy the sentence that tells the main idea of the story.**

1. After the fight with the tyrannosaur, some triceratops acted as if nothing had happened.

2. When the tyrannosaur was on the ground, one of the triceratops charged and struck it in the side of the head.

3. Tekla received cracked bones and an infection from a battle with a tyrannosaur.

4. When Tekla became an adult, she did not run from predators the way she did as a juvenile.

_____

_____

_____

1

1. It was instinct that led the male triceratops to fight to see who would mate.

    What did that instinct ensure? _____

    _____

2. What did Tekla always do after laying eggs?

    _____

3. Did a mother triceratops raise her young? _____

4. How are human parents different from triceratops parents?

    _____

5. How old was Tekla when she had her last fight? _____

6. Why did Tekla run from the tyrannosaur at first?

    _____

7. What told Tekla to stop and fight the tyrannosaur? _____

8. How does pain serve intelligent animals?

    _____

9. For how long did dinosaurs inhabit the earth?

    _____

10. How much would a full-grown triceratops weigh? _____

2 Fill in each blank using a word in the box.

| stampeding | offspring | urge |
| concealed | faked | trample |

1. The black kittens are the _____ of the brown cat.

2. A loud noise frightened the herd into _____.

3. Willie fixed dinner because he had an _____ to eat.

3 Write the parts for each word.

1. substandard = _____ + _____

2. disorderly = _____ + _____ + _____

3. subtracted = _____ + _____ + _____

4. reminder = _____ + _____ + _____

1

1. Did Tekla seem to feel a lot of pain when she died? _____

2. How did Tekla's attacker die?

_____

3. Why weren't the bones of Tekla and the tyrannosaur eaten by scavengers?

_____

_____

4. What happened to the bones of the two dinosaurs?

_____

5. How long after the dinosaurs became extinct did humans inhabit the earth?

_____

6. What has happened to the crust of the earth since that time? _____

_____

7. What does a paleontologist study?

_____

8. In what part of the United States did the paleontologists find Tekla's bones?

_____

9. How did the paleontologists know the triceratops had been in fights?

_____

_____

10. Is the story of Tekla all true or is some of it made up?

_____

2 **Fill in each blank using a word in the box.**

pounced	preserved	silt
buckled	paleontologist	fossil

1. _____ covered the bottom of the muddy pond.

2. Pepe was a _____ who studied dinosaurs.

3. The ancient mummy was well _____.

1

1. What is a champion?

_____

_____

2. Name an official list of records.

_____

3. What kinds of records are people interested in? _____

_____

4. Why is an authoritative listing of records useful?

_____

_____

5. What record is held by the Guinness record book?

_____

6. Why does the author say the Guinness book is fascinating?

_____

_____

7. Name three records that could be called accidents of nature.

_____

_____

8. Why do some people want to set records?

_____

_____

_____

9. Name three unusual sports in the Guinness book of records.

_____

_____

_____

10. What interesting question did the joke-telling record suggest?

_____

_____

2   **Fill in each blank using a word in the box.**

champion	pounced	record
fossilized	buckled	official

1. He set a _____ for the quickest time.

2. The fastest runner was the _____ of the contest.

3. The president made an _____ statement to reporters.

Errors

1

1. What was Milly's job? _____

2. What was Milly's one serious fault? _____

   _____

3. What games was Milly good at?

   _____

4. Milly made Fred Frankle say something in baby talk. What did he say?

   _____

5. What kind of beams was Milly working with? _____

6. What did Milly do with the results of her experiments?

   _____

7. What does the heat of a laser beam do to a metal?

   _____

8. Which metal gave a strange reading on the metal detector? _____

9. Why did Fred think Milly should stop telling jokes?

   _____

   _____

10. Why didn't Milly want to stop telling jokes?

   _____

Lesson
56

2 Fill in each blank using a word in the box.

| property | physics | fault |
| transformed | detect | device |

1. Essie couldn't _____ the faint odor.

2. The witch _____ the handsome prince into a frog.

3. Arthur has a nice personality except for one _____.

3 Copy the sentence that tells the main idea of the story.

1. When Milly Jacobson conducted experiments, she carefully recorded the results.

2. Milly Jacobson was good at playing tennis, bowling, and shooting pool.

3. Milly Jacobson had been experimenting with laser beams, trying to discover some of the basic properties of metals.

4. Milly Jacobson was an intelligent professor of physics who loved to play practical jokes on other professors.

_____

_____

_____

4 Write the parts for each word.

1. researcher = _____ + _____ + _____

2. submerge = _____ + _____

3. triangle = _____ + _____

4. disinterested = _____ + _____ + _____

Copyright © SRA/McGraw-Hill. All rights reserved.

Lesson 56 **99**

1 1. Why do you think physicists want to talk to others in their field?

_____

2. What did Milly become at a convention? _____

3. What three tricks did Milly pack?

a. _____

b. _____

c. _____

4. What was Milly scheduled to talk about? _____

_____

5. What wasn't Milly ready to talk about? _____

_____

6. Who went to the convention with Milly? _____

7. What trick did Milly play on Fred at the airport?

_____

_____

8. What do you think of the trick Milly played on Fred?

_____

_____

9. What did Milly lie about?

_____

2 **Fill in each blank using a word in the box.**

researcher	physicist	jokester
bonds	physics	property

1. Millie worked in the field of physics. That made her a _____.

2. The molecules of metals are held together by strong _____.

3. Carmen loved to discover new facts, so she decided to be

   a _____ in physics.

1

1. In what city was the physicists' convention being held? _____

2. What kind of person was Dr. Terrance? _____

3. What trick did Milly play on Dr. Terrance?

_____

_____

4. Why did the cue stick make an extra-loud bang?

_____

5. What trick did Milly play on a "very prominent physicist"?

_____

_____

6. How did the professor from Virginia introduce Milly?

_____

_____

7. What trick did Milly play on the audience?

_____

_____

8. How do you know Milly was well received by the audience?

_____

_____

9. Give two reasons why Milly enjoyed the convention.

a. _____

b. _____

2 **Fill in each blank using a word in the box.**

harmless	formal	researcher
bonds	prominent	delicately

1. A garter snake isn't poisonous, so it's really _____.

2. She handled the vase _____ so she wouldn't break it.

3. Wherever the _____ man went, people knew who he was.

1

1. When did Milly play most of her jokes at the convention?

_____

2. What was one reason people found Milly so funny?

_____

_____

3. Why did Milly start planning her tricks for next year's convention?

_____

4. Why wouldn't Milly play practical jokes on her students?

_____

_____

_____

5. Why did she think it was all right to play jokes on other professors?

_____

_____

6. What was wrong with the piece of zinc Milly was experimenting with?

_____

7. How did Milly turn the tables on Fred over the zinc?

_____

_____

8. What did Fred mean when he said Milly was incurable?

_____

_____

9. What did Milly put in the box with the gold? _____

10. Why did Milly think she could find gold with the laser?

_____

_____

2 **Fill in each blank using a word in the box.**

impish	undergraduate	graduate student
doctoral degree	related to	incurable

1. The work they did was _____ the surprise they planned.

2. Hector stayed in school until he finally got his _____.

3. The _____ monkey threw a pie in her master's face.

3 **Write the parts for each word.**

1. preserve   = _____ + _____

2. subside   = _____ + _____

3. unprofessionally = _____ + _____ + _____

4. rewarmed   = _____ + _____ + _____

1

1. What is one of the more popular record topics?

_____

2. What is the fastest recorded time for a human to run 100 meters?

_____

3. What is the fastest marine animal to be scientifically clocked?

_____

4. What is the fastest land animal?

_____

5. Is it easier to measure the speed of land animals or the speed of marine animals?

_____

6. How fast can a spine-tailed swift fly?

_____

7. Which is faster, the diving speed or the flying speed of the falcon?

_____

8. Name two machines that go faster than any creature.

_____

9. What is the speed record for the fastest machine in this story?

_____

2 **Fill in each blank using a word in the box.**

fascinated	attained	breed
incurable	surpassed	prominent

1. They continued climbing until they _____ their goal.

2. Sonia _____ all other running times to set a new record.

3. Cats are _____ by mice.

1 1. What did Milly order to conduct her experiment?

_____

_____

2. **Here are the things Milly did before she phoned in her order for dirt and gravel. Number the things 1, 2, 3, and 4 to show the order in which she did them.**

_____ a. repeated the experiment

_____ b. tested the gold

_____ c. got a garbage can

_____ d. recorded the metal detector readings

3. Why was Fred sarcastic?

_____

_____

4. Where were the piles of dirt and gravel?

_____

5. What did Milly put in the garbage can?

_____

6. How much did the laser gun weigh?

_____

7. a. Did other metals in the pile affect Milly's results? _____

b. Why? _____

_____

8. Why did Milly say to herself, "Don't jump to any conclusions"?

_____

_____

9. What machine did Milly use to check her calculations?

_____

10. What metal could the metal detector identify even when other metals were present?

_____

2 Fill in each blank using a word in the box.

sarcastic	apparatus	data
calculated	identify	breed

1. No one could _____ Joe when he was wearing his gorilla costume.

2. The scientist _____ the speed at which the freeway traffic was moving.

3. She smiled as she spoke, but her voice was very _____ and mean.

3 Copy the sentence that tells the main idea of the story.

1. Milly tested her laser device and discovered that it could detect small pieces of gold in a pile of dirt.

2. Milly and four others moved the laser machine outside and pointed it toward the pile of dirt.

3. A truck dumped two huge piles of dirt in front of the physics lab.

4. The signal from the metal detector became weaker and weaker as more dirt surrounded the piece of gold in the pile.

_____

_____

_____

Errors

1

1. Where did Milly plan to go look for gold?

_____

2. What kind of recreational vehicle did Milly rent?

_____

3. Why couldn't the guide she hired do much walking? _____

_____

4. How did Milly talk the man in the machine shop into making the mounting fast?

_____

5. How was Milly's research with the laser paid for? _____

_____

6. What trick had Milly played on Dr. Jenkins the year before?

_____

_____

_____

7. Why do you think the dean didn't believe Milly was serious?

_____

_____

8. How much money did the dean think this trick of Milly's would cost?

_____

9. How did Milly convince the dean to approve the requests?

_____

_____

10. What did the dean promise Milly? _____

_____

2 **Fill in each blank using a word in the box.**

mounted	requests	vehicle
salary	recommended	identify

1. They _____ the statue on a big marble base.

2. Irene asked for a raise in her _____.

3. The doctor _____ that he go on a diet.

3 **Write the parts for each word.**

1. careless = _____ + _____

2. requesting = _____ + _____ + _____

3. meaningless = _____ + _____ + _____

4. heartless = _____ + _____

1. What prevented Milly from seeing the mountains?

   _____

2. Who helped Milly mount the laser on the pickup truck?

   _____

3. What was the name of the guide Milly had hired? _____

4. What kind of clothes was the guide wearing?

   _____

   _____

5. What was his dog's name? _____

6. Why had Mr. Hicks chosen that name for his dog? _____

   _____

   _____

7. How did Milly predict what Mr. Hicks would look like?

   _____

   _____

8. Why did Mr. Hicks laugh when Milly said she had a gold-finding device?

   _____

   _____

9. How do most gold prospectors make money?

   _____

   _____

10. What is a glory hole?

   _____

2 **Fill in each blank using a word in the box.**

shrugged	approval	arranged
indicator	scurried	requests

1. Before they could go on their camping trip, they had to get their parents'

   _____.

2. After scurrying around, they _____ to take the five o'clock
   plane to Hawaii.

3. The cat _____ across the basement floor.

Errors

1

1. Why did Milly keep looking out the back window of the truck?

   _____

   _____

2. What did Mr. Hicks think of the laser?

   _____

3. How much gold did Mr. Hicks say you could get in a day if you panned a stream?

   _____

4. How much would that amount of gold be worth?

   _____

5. What are the two parts of a sluice?

   a. _____

   b. _____

6. Where did the miners hope to find gold—in the sand or in the water?

   _____

7. Why didn't the miners want to move their sluice?

   _____

8. a. Do you think Milly will get the miners to change their minds? _____

   b. If yes, how? _____

   _____

9. What warning did Milly give Mr. Hicks and the miners?

   _____

   _____

10. Why did the miners and Mr. Hicks laugh at Milly? _____

_____

_____

2 **Fill in each blank using a word in the box.**

impressively	rig	trough
speck	hailed	amusing

1. The clown was very _____.

2. Georgia had a bothersome _____ of dirt in her eye.

3. The champion talked _____ about his power.

1. In which state is Mount Whitney found? _____

2. What are the conterminous states? _____

_____

_____

3. What is the highest mountain in the conterminous states?

_____

4. Name the states in which the following mountains are found.

   a. Mauna Kea _____

   b. Mount Rainier _____

   c. Mount Shasta _____

   d. Mount McKinley _____

5. Which two mountains named in the article were once active volcanoes?

_____

6. What is the highest mountain in North America? _____

7. What is the highest mountain on earth? _____

8. What kind of injuries have several climbers of Mount Everest suffered?

_____

_____

9. Which mountain is highest from base to summit? _____

10. Why is Half Dome an impressive-looking mountain?

_____

_____

2 **Fill in each blank using a word in the box.**

peak	sea level	volcano
amused	sheer	amazement

1. When you sit on an ocean beach, you are at _____.

2. The liquid rock from the _____ almost destroyed the village.

3. The mountain climber hung on to a _____ slope.

3 **Write the parts for each word.**

1. thoughtless = _____ + _____

2. displaying = _____ + _____ + _____

3. presenter = _____ + _____ + _____

4. regardless = _____ + _____

1

1. Why was Milly irritated at the beginning of this story?

   _____

   _____

2. How did Milly get Mr. Hicks to start digging?

   _____

   _____

3. Why did Mr. Hicks say, "Unless of course that nugget is in China"?

   _____

   _____

4. How much sand did Mr. Hicks shovel out before Milly found the nugget?

   _____

5. Was the first piece of gold very big? _____

6. What made Milly start daydreaming?

   _____

7. How much gold had Milly promised to find for the men?

   _____

8. How many nuggets did Milly find with her laser beam? _____

9. In what ways did the men act differently after Milly found the gold?

   _____

   _____

10. Where did the truck go after Milly and Mr. Hicks left the men? _____

    _____

2 **Fill in each blank using a word in the box.**

irritated	antics	express
scan	dismantled	manner

1. Marcos laughed at the clown's _____.

2. When the machine was _____, it was just a pile of gears and springs.

3. She talked in an impatient _____.

Errors

1

1. Why was Milly getting excited as the truck went up alongside the stream?

   _____

   _____

   _____

2. Why did Mr. Hicks have to stop the truck? _____

   _____

   _____

   _____

3. Why did Milly get dizzy?

   _____

4. How did Mr. Hicks know there was gold somewhere up that stream?

   _____

   _____

5. How many times did they move the truck? _____

6. How far did they move the truck each time?

   _____

7. What other instrument besides the laser beam did Milly use?

   _____

8. How deep in the rock was the gold buried? _____

9. What are they going to have to use to get the gold out? _____

10. Why did Mr. Hicks hesitate to use dynamite?

   _____

2 **Fill in each blank using a word in the box.**

adventurous	reliable	cascading
grade	calculator	estimate

1. He added the numbers on his _____.

2. The car rolled down the steep _____.

3. The investigator made an _____ about the cost of repairs.

1

1. How deep in the rock was the gold buried? _____

2. Why was Mr. Hicks worried about the blasting job?

   _____

   _____

3. How many holes did Mr. Hicks chisel? _____

4. How far was each hole from the one closest to it? _____

5. How many sticks of dynamite did Mr. Hicks place in the first hole? _____

6. How would Elmer Tooley have done the blasting?

   _____

   _____

7. Why do you think Mr. Hicks connected a long wick to the three dynamite sticks?

   _____

   _____

8. Why did Milly have to go uphill? _____

9. Why did Mr. Hicks drive the truck downhill instead of uphill?

   _____

   _____

10. What effect did the blast have on the rock?

    _____

    _____

2 **Fill in each blank using a word in the box.**

| shorings | chisel | wick |
| impatient | enlarged | assured |

1. She lit the candle's _____.

2. He became _____ after waiting all day for his package.

3. The picture was _____ to fill the entire wall.

3 **Write the parts for each word.**

1. straightness = _____ + _____

2. expressing = _____ + _____ + _____

3. remarked = _____ + _____ + _____

4. unselfishness = _____ + _____ + _____

1. What did the second blast do to the rock? _____

_____

2. How many sticks of dynamite did Mr. Hicks set for the third blast? _____

3. Why do you think Milly and Mr. Hicks were scared after the third blast?

_____

_____

_____

4. Why couldn't Milly see where she was going?

_____

5. What did the glory hole look like? _____

_____

6. What was the gold deposit shaped like?

_____

7. How wide was the gold deposit at its thickest place?

_____

8. What adjective did Mr. Hicks use three times to describe his feelings about the glory

hole? _____

9. What did Doctor do when Mr. Hicks kissed Doctor?

_____

_____

10. How did Milly act at the end of this story? _____

_____

2 **Fill in each blank using a word in the box.**

| glistening | assured | scarcely |
| brilliance | flask | initial |

1. It was so dark that she could _____ see.

2. The water was _____ in the sunshine.

3. He took a long drink of water from his _____.

3 **Copy the sentence that tells the main idea of the story.**

1. Mr. Hicks jumped up and down, kissed the rock, and then kissed the dog.

2. After the third blast, part of the mountain slid into the stream below.

3. Mr. Hicks blasted away part of the mountainside, revealing gold.

4. Mr. Hicks had never seen a glory hole before.

_____

_____

Errors

1

1. Who set more National Basketball Association records than any other player?

   _____

2. What will a malfunction of the pituitary gland cause?

   _____

3. Who is the tallest woman on record? _____

4. Where was the tallest woman born?

   _____

5. Who is the tallest man on record? _____

6. What was the height of the tallest man on record?

   _____

7. a. Could the tallest man on record stand up in an average room? _____

   b. Explain. _____

   _____

8. Could Zeng Jinlian stand up in the average room? _____

9. Who was the smallest full-grown adult?

   _____

 2 **Fill in each blank using a word in the box.**

| scarcely | coordinated | exaggerated |
| glands | abnormally | brilliance |

1. A team must be _____ to perform well.

2. "I wasn't lying!" the little girl said. "I just _____ a little."

3. The tiny squirrel was _____ small.

1

1. On what kind of land can people file a mining claim?

_____

2. How many acres can they claim? _____

3. When can they claim more acres than that?

_____

4. What is the problem in marking off a claim? _____

_____

_____

5. **Here are several things Mr. Hicks did to mark the claim.**
   Number the things 1, 2, 3, and 4 to show the order in which he did them.

   _____ a. measured about three hundred yards along the cliff

   _____ b. took a roll of string from the pickup

   _____ c. marked the claim on the map

   _____ d. measured the distance from the stream to the cliff

6. Mr. Hicks marked the claim so that the glory hole was _____

_____.

7. Why was it easy for Mr. Hicks to mark the claim?

_____

8. What did the note in the tin can say?

_____

_____

9. How did Milly want the claim divided?

_____

_____

_____

10. Why do you think Milly gave her claim away?

_____

_____

2 Fill in each blank using a word in the box.

mineral	greedy	stunts
nudge	area	veins

1. The _____ child took all the cookies.

2. Ellen explored the entire _____ around the camp.

3. The rocks had rich _____ of gold in them.

3 Write the parts for each word.

1. awareness = _____ + _____

2. renewed = _____ + _____ + _____

3. broadly = _____ + _____

4. subheading = _____ + _____ + _____

Lesson 72

1

1. Why were big game hunters once welcomed in African villages?

   _____

   _____

2. What five African animals were considered to be the most dangerous to hunt?

   _____

   _____

3. What do grazing animals eat? _____

4. What do predators eat? _____

5. Why do African animals have good defenses?

   _____

   _____

   _____

6. a. How much can an African elephant weigh? _____

   b. How long are its tusks? _____

   c. How fast can it run? _____

7. Why is a wounded elephant dangerous to hunt?

   _____

   _____

8. What do you think happened to the wild animals when large farms were fenced off and planted in Africa?

   _____

   _____

9. Why do you think many animals are in danger of become extinct?

_____

_____

10. a. Do you think big game hunters would be welcome in Africa today? _____

b. Explain._____

_____

_____

2 Fill in each blank using a word in the box.

extinct	reduced	capable
resident	deceive	greedy

1. He _____ the amount of food he ate.

2. The dinosaur is an _____ animal.

3. The wall was not _____ of stopping the tidal wave.

Errors

1

1. What is the only animal that will make an African elephant retreat? _____

2. What are the three reasons the elephant is not the most dangerous African animal to hunt?

   a. _____

   b. _____

   c. _____

3. What three features make the lion an expert predator?

   a. _____

   b. _____

   c. _____
   _____

4. a. Did lions become expert predators just so they could kill people? _____

   b. Explain. _____
   _____

5. What three weapons does the lion use?

   a. _____

   b. _____

   c. _____

6. The lion lives in a group called a _____.

7. How many hours does a lion sleep each day? _____

8. Why is it easy for a hunter to find a lion in the brush?

_____

_____

9. a. Would a hunter use the same gun to kill elephants and lions? _____

b. Explain. _____

_____

10. Give two reasons why a hunter might want to kill an elephant or a lion.

_____

_____

_____

2 **Fill in each blank using a word in the box.**

retreated	evolution	strides
enormous	extinct	hurtle

1. The cat _____ from the dog.

2. The child couldn't keep up when her father walked with long _____.

3. The triceratops grew and grew until it was _____.

Errors

1

1. How much can a rhinoceros weigh?

_____

2. How fast can it run? _____

3. What two animals in these stories use their horns to defend themselves?

_____

4. How are a rhinoceros's horns different from an elephant's tusks?

_____

_____

_____

5. Why does a rhinoceros need tickbirds? _____

_____

6. a. Which African animals live together in a relationship that helps them both?

_____

   b. Explain. _____

_____

_____

7. What senses are highly developed in the Cape buffalo?

_____

8. With what animals do people often confuse the African Cape buffalo?

_____

9. Write **predator** or **grazing animal** after the name of each animal.

a. lion _____

b. elephant _____

c. tyrannosaur _____

d. triceratops _____

10. What strategy does the Cape buffalo use to defend itself against a lion?

_____

_____

2 **Fill in each blank using a word in the box.**

ill-tempered	confused	matted
glance	strategy	remarkably

1. The mixed-up instructions _____ Betsy.

2. The day was _____ warm and pretty.

3. The _____ horse kicked his trainer.

3 **1.** frequently = _____ + _____

2. unfitness = _____ + _____ + _____

3. discussed = _____ + _____ + _____

4. actually = _____ + _____

Errors

1

1. What is the name of the fastest snake? _____

2. How fast can the fastest snake travel? _____

   _____

3. How high a wall can the fastest snake climb? _____

4. How do constrictors kill their prey?

   _____

5. What is the name of the longest snake ever found?

   _____

6. What is the most poisonous ocean snake? _____

7. Where are both the most poisonous snakes of the ocean and of the land found?

   _____

8. What is the longest poisonous snake? _____

9. Why does a cobra appear to sway to the music of a snake charmer?

   _____

   _____

10. Name two poisonous snakes found near New Orleans.

   _____

2   **Fill in each blank using a word in the box.**

trance	modified	venom
comparison	coiled	aggressive

1. Jacob gets in fights because he is so _____.

2. The cowboys _____ their ropes into loops.

3. She was so sleepy that she seemed to be in a _____.

Errors

1

1. Name four ways a Cape buffalo is more dangerous than a rhinoceros when it charges.

   a. _____

   b. _____

   c. _____

   d. _____

   _____

2. Why are professional big game hunters required to track down wounded Cape buffalos

   and kill them? _____

   _____

3. Why have some professional big game hunters lost their licenses to hunt?

   _____

   _____

4. What is the most dangerous African animal to hunt? _____

   _____

5. How much does a leopard weigh?

   _____

6. a. Which African animal is most closely related to the leopard? _____

   b. Explain. _____

   _____

7. What does a leopard look like? _____

   _____

8. The leopard has more _____ in relation to its _____
   than nearly any other animal.

9. Name two things a leopard uses to defend itself against the hunter.

_____

10. What is wrong with a jungle movie that shows a person winning out over a leopard in a

wrestling match? _____

_____

_____

2 **Fill in each blank using a word in the box.**

range	efficient	determined
rescue	instantly	relation

1. An _____ cheetah doesn't waste movements when it runs.

2. Hugo's mind was made up. He was _____ that he would get
a job.

3. In _____ to its size, the leopard has more strength than any
other animal.

1

1. What does a leopard like to do most of the day?

   _____

2. What does the leopard sometimes hunt on the plain?

   _____

3. Where does a hunter have to go to find the leopard?

   _____

4. Why is a leopard almost invisible in the forest? _____

   _____

   _____

5. Why is it easy for a hunter to find a lion in the brush?

   _____

   _____

6. Why is it not easy for a hunter to find a leopard in the brush?

   _____

   _____

7. The leopard has more _____ in relation to its _____
   than nearly any other animal.

8. Why is the leopard considered the most dangerous African animal to hunt?

   _____

   _____

   _____

9. a. Do you think the leopard would attack any of the other animals described in these

stories? _____

b. Explain. _____

_____

_____

10. Other animals have coloring that makes them hard to see. Name some of those animals.

_____

2 **Fill in each blank using a word in the box.**

downed	disadvantage	created
filtered	advantage	instantly

1. The gazelle was at a _____ because of its injured leg.

2. The two birds _____ a loud noise.

3. He _____ the silt out of the muddy water.

3 **Write the parts for each word.**

1. presenting = _____ + _____ + _____

2. unfiltered = _____ + _____ + _____

3. returnable = _____ + _____ + _____

4. preventable = _____ + _____ + _____

1 1. Why do wild animals kill?

_____

2. How do people hunt the leopard unfairly? _____

_____

_____

3. How do people hunt the Cape buffalo unfairly?

_____

_____

4. Why does the rhinoceros attack?

_____

5. How many leopards once lived in Africa? _____

6. How many leopards are left? _____

7. What animal kills with no good reason? _____

8. a. Are people the most dangerous animals in the world? _____

   b. Explain. _____

   _____

   _____

9. a. Do you think these stories are in favor of big game hunting? _____

   b. Explain. _____

   _____

   _____

10. a. Is there a time when people should be allowed to kill wild African animals?

_____

b. Explain. _____

_____

_____

2 **Fill in each blank using a word in the box.**

intruder	instantly	apparent
required	concerned	puny

1. When Amanda cried, it was _____ that she was sad.

2. The nurse was _____ with the patient's health.

3. Lemons are _____ if you want to make lemonade.

Errors

1

1. What did Milly do as soon as she got back to the university?

   _____

2. What was the title of the paper? _____

   _____

3. Where did Milly want to present the paper? _____

   _____

4. How soon was the convention scheduled? _____

5. Why couldn't Milly just show up at the convention with her paper?

   _____

   _____

6. When did Milly first fall asleep at her desk?

   _____

   _____

7. When Milly finished the first draft of her paper, what did she do?

   _____

8. Why was it a nice coincidence that Milly wanted to present a paper at the convention?

   _____

9. Why did Milly call herself a show-off? _____

   _____

   _____

10. What did Milly say to Fred each time he nagged her about her trip to California?

    _____

2 **Fill in each blank using a word in the box.**

reactions	presentation	referring
duplicated	nagging	coincidence

1. Milly made a _____ to the other scientists.

2. Rob got mad when Bart kept _____ him.

3. The artist's portrait exactly _____ the subject.

1 1. Is the whole human race growing taller? _____

2. Explain what is meant by a "genetic" characteristic.

_____

_____

3. Name one genetic characteristic. _____

4. How far back does a human being's genetic inheritance go?

_____

5. What effect does inheritance have on growth? _____

_____

6. What is another important thing that influences growth?

_____

7. What is nutrition? _____

_____

8. What happened to people who lived during long periods of starvation?

_____

_____

9. How tall were ancient people?

_____

10. How do we know how tall ancient people were?

_____

2 Fill in each blank using a word in the box.

ancient	genetic	retreat
starvation	plentiful	evolution

1. Breadfruit will be _____ when it gets ripe.

2. The pattern of growth that a child inherits from its parents is a

   _____ growth pattern.

3. She wasn't just old; she was _____.

3 Write the parts for each word.

1. discharge = _____ + _____

2. unreadable = _____ + _____ + _____

3. preserve = _____ + _____

4. redesigned = _____ + _____ + _____

Errors

1

1. Where was the International Convention of Physicists to be held?

   _____

2. Why didn't Fred want Milly to go to the convention?

   _____

   _____

3. What delayed the plane? _____

4. What was different about Milly's preparation for this convention?

   _____

5. Why did they have to get a new room for Milly's meeting?

   _____

6. Why do you think so many people came to Milly's meeting?

   _____

   _____

7. What did the first speaker talk about? _____

8. What was the title of Milly's paper? _____

   _____

9. How did the audience react to the title of Milly's paper?

   _____

10. Once Fred said to Milly, "You're like the little child who hollered wolf too many times." How is that statement coming true now?

    _____

    _____

    _____

2 **Fill in each blank using a word in the box.**

hassling	peeved	acoustics
mineral	podium	coincidence

1. The _____ in the concert hall were very good.

2. He gave his presentation from behind a _____.

3. When you keep nagging, I really get _____.

1

1. What happened every time Milly began to say something?

_____

2. What did the moderator finally ask the audience to do?

_____

3. How did Milly summarize her discovery? _____

_____

_____

_____

4. What slides did Milly show?

_____

5. What was the one question asked during the presentation? _____

_____

6. What was the yell that greeted the showing of the laser gun?

_____

7. Why did Milly want someone to take the gold nugget behind the concrete wall?

_____

_____

8. Who volunteered to go behind the wall with the nugget? _____

9. Where did Milly first aim the laser gun?

_____

10. What trick did the audience think Milly was playing with the laser gun?

_____

2 **Fill in each blank using a word in the box.**

summary	modified	formulas
confirm	routine	interrupted

1. He made a short _____ of his whole presentation.

2. As part of her daily _____, Sarah bought a newspaper.

3. She _____ him in the middle of his sentence.

1. What had the laser gun done to the wall and the room?

_____

_____

2. How many foot-lengths from the end of the hall was the nugget? _____

3. How close to the nugget was the spot the laser beam had picked out?

_____

4. Who was suspected of being part of the gag? _____

5. Why couldn't Milly promise to find a piece of iron behind the concrete wall?

_____

6. Milly's laser beam and metal detector could only distinguish between

_____ and _____.

7. Why do you think one man wanted to place the gold piece himself?

_____

8. What did one physicist think Milly might have done to the piece of gold she used?

_____

9. As this story ends, how are members of the audience getting ready to test Milly's claims?

_____

_____

_____

2 **Fill in each blank using a word in the box.**

typical	adequate	ducts
reinforced	distinguish	proceeded

1. The hiker _____ down the long trail.

2. They were hungry because they hadn't eaten _____ food.

3. You could _____ Spot from Rover because Spot had spots and Rover did not.

3 **Write the parts for each word.**

1. unworldly = _____ + _____ + _____

2. recording = _____ + _____ + _____

3. seriousness = _____ + _____

4. disappoint = _____ + _____

Errors

1

1. Where in California did Milly find the glory hole?

_____

2. Who helped Milly stake her claim to the glory hole? _____

3. Here are three gold objects that Milly identified.
   Number them **1, 2,** and **3** to show the order in which she identified them.

   _____ a. a necklace

   _____ b. a ring

   _____ c. a pocket watch

4. How did the crowd at Milly's meeting get so large that people had to stand?

_____

_____

5. How much was the glory hole worth?

_____

6. What did Milly plan to do with the money?

_____

_____

_____

7. What was Milly's reward?

_____

_____

8. What could Milly do if she decided she wanted gold after all?

_____

_____

9. What was the biggest day in Milly's life?

_____

_____

10. What is Milly doing now?

_____

2 **Fill in each blank using a word in the box.**

technical	trance	subsided
refused	ducts	incurable

1. When the storm _____, they closed their umbrellas.

2. Bess got mad when Ben _____ to let her use his bike.

3. The professor provided _____ information about the laser equipment.

Errors

1 1. In this passage, a wave 112 feet high was compared with a building. How many stories

tall is that building? _____

2. What are two causes of high waves? _____

3. Why don't wind-pushed waves grow as high as waves caused by earthquakes?

_____

4. How fast can an earthquake-caused wave travel?

_____

5. What does a wave caused by an earthquake do when it comes near the shore?

_____

6. What happens to a wave when water keeps moving and climbing over the water that

has slowed down? _____

_____

7. What caused a wave of 220 feet in 1964?

_____

8. What causes tides?

_____

9. When are the tides the strongest?

_____

_____

10. Where would you have to be to see the strongest tide in the world?

_____

2 **Fill in each blank using a word in the box.**

| plunged | hurl | plumes |
| gale | tides | exceeded |

1. The car _____ the speed limit.

2. Every day, the ocean's _____ cause the water level to rise and fall.

3. She _____ from the diving board into the pool.

1

1. Who lived with Agnes Lark?

_____

2. Why did Agnes and her companions live in the kitchen?

_____

_____

3. Why didn't Agnes have many occasions to defend her junk?

_____

4. How was Agnes awakened every morning?

_____

5. What did Agnes do as soon as she got up? _____

_____

6. Describe the dog Edison.

_____

_____

7. What did Agnes do when she took breaks from her work? _____

_____

8. List three of Agnes's unsuccessful inventions.

_____

_____

_____

9. Why couldn't Agnes admit to herself that her inventions didn't work?

_____

_____

10. What did Agnes invent that could have changed the history of the world?

_____

2 **Fill in each blank using a word in the box.**

| inhabitants | insisted | invented |
| unconvincing | exceed | referred |

1. The _____ of the house were not at home.

2. The scientist _____ many new devices.

3. Felipa _____ on going to the circus Wednesday.

3 **Copy the sentence that tells the main idea of the story.**

1. Agnes lived on the outskirts of Redmond in a house filled with junk.

2. Agnes was an elderly woman who had invented over three hundred things that didn't work.

3. Agnes had a cat named Einstein and a dog named Edison.

4. When Agnes took a break, she loved to walk to the store or putter in her garden.

_____

_____

_____

4 **Write the parts for each word.**

1. uncertainly = _____ + _____ + _____

2. unbreakable = _____ + _____ + _____

3. socially = _____ + _____

4. hopeless = _____ + _____

Errors

1

1. How fast do electromagnetic waves travel through space?

   _____

2. The longest electromagnetic waves are known as _____.

3. What does a radio wave become when it is made shorter? _____

4. What kind of wave is used in a microwave oven? _____

5. As a heat wave is made shorter, what kind of wave does it become?

   _____

6. The longest light wave is seen as what color? _____

7. What color of the rainbow is produced by the shortest light wave? _____

8. Each of the letters below stands for a color in the rainbow. In each blank, write the color for the letter.

   R _____   B _____

   O _____   I _____

   Y _____   V _____

   G _____

9. What kind of wave causes sunburn? _____

10. Why do people who run X-ray machines stand behind a lead plate?

    _____

2 **Fill in each blank using a word in the box.**

crest	penetrated	electromagnetic
unconvincing	invention	insist

1. A surfer balances his board on the _____ of the wave.

2. The pin _____ the balloon.

3. _____ waves travel through space very quickly.

1

1. Which waves are longer than light waves but shorter than radio waves?

   _____

2. Are X rays shorter or longer than ultraviolet waves? _____

3. What were the shortest electromagnetic waves known before Agnes Lark invented the

   dop machine? _____

4. What was wrong with the garage door that could be opened by a CB radio?

   _____

   _____

5. What happened when Agnes tried to pull her hand from the TV screen?

   _____

6. What was the first message that Agnes received through the dop machine?

   _____

7. How did Agnes feel during her first dop experience?

   _____

8. What happened when Agnes turned off the electric motor?

   _____

9. Who sent Agnes the first dop message? _____

10. Name the colors of the rainbow. _____

    _____

2 Fill in each blank using a word in the box.

failures	indeed	whir
tug	panic	prickly

1. The sun will _____ rise tomorrow.

2. The frightened hunter tried not to _____.

3. The first airplanes were _____ because they couldn't get off
   the ground.

1. What was Agnes arguing with herself about at the beginning of this story?

_____

_____

2. There were two sides to Agnes's argument. What were they?

   a. _____

   _____

   _____

   b. _____

   _____

   _____

3. What does the word "gamble" mean? _____

4. What second thoughts did Agnes have after picking up the screwdriver the second time?

_____

_____

5. In what way was the screwdriver like a TV antenna?

_____

_____

6. What was Agnes's first message?

_____

_____

7. From whom do you think the first message came? _____

8. Who was talking to himself in the second message Agnes received?

_____

9. What was the message that Agnes received just before turning off the machine?

_____

_____

_____

2 **Fill in each blank using a word in the box.**

| anxiety | famous | conscious |
| occasionally | risk | indifferently |

1. I feel _____, and my palms sweat just before I take a test.

2. Julia was _____ of the faucet dripping.

3. Even years after Manuel moved away, he _____ thought about his old school.

3 **Write the parts for each word.**

1. precooked = _____ + _____ + _____

2. reworking = _____ + _____ + _____

3. waveless = _____ + _____

4. untrained = _____ + _____ + _____

Errors

1

1. Which animals are most like human beings? _____

_____

2. Which would probably weigh more, a full-grown chimpanzee or an average adult

human male? _____

3. In what way are chimpanzees extremely strong? _____

_____

4. Which usually live longer, human beings or great apes? _____

5. What is the longest great apes have been known to live? _____

6. Which kind of great ape is the heaviest? _____

7. Which are more intelligent, people or great apes? _____

8. Why can't great apes learn to speak like people? _____

_____

9. What did the scientists teach Washoe so that she could express ideas?

_____

10. What do the scientists who worked with Washoe think about the way she used sign

language? _____

_____

2 **Fill in each blank using a word in the box.**

intrigued	image	capacity
accurate	personality	focused

1. The painting showed a faint _____ of cows on a farm.

2. Luis is friendly; he has a nice _____.

3. The gas tank had a _____ of eleven gallons.

1

1. What did the letters in "dop" stand for?

_____

2. What did the dop machine display?

_____

3. Where did the dop machine display these things?

_____

4. What did Agnes discover was the best antenna for the dop machine?

_____

_____

5. Why could Agnes have become the most famous quiz show contestant in television history?

_____

_____

_____

6. How could Agnes have become a famous gambler?

_____

_____

7. What did Agnes want to become publicly recognized as?

_____

8. a. How much did the attorney want as an initial fee?

_____

   b. What would the fee pay for?

_____

9. How did the lawyer treat Agnes?

_____

_____

2 **Fill in each blank using a word in the box.**

associated	transmitted	productive
patent	assume	incurred

1. Marco _____ his new idea to the other students.

2. The _____ chicken laid many eggs.

3. When it is very cloudy, I _____ that it will rain.

1

1. Why did Agnes want to win money at blackjack? _____

_____

2. Why wouldn't the man at the museum door let Agnes into the science society meeting?

_____

3. How did Agnes feel the morning after her bad dream?

_____

_____

4. What gave Agnes the idea of being a detective?

_____

5. Why did Agnes want to know if the robbery suspect was going to be on television?

_____

_____

6. Why do you think the police officer was rude to Agnes?

_____

_____

7. How did Agnes try to make contact with the suspect?

_____

_____

8. Who do you think was having the thoughts that came to Agnes in the first message?

_____

_____

9. What did Agnes find out about the file cabinet problem?

_____

10. How did Agnes know she was close to contacting the suspect?

_____

_____

2 Fill in each blank using a word in the box.

superb	process	approached
lingered	attentive	humiliating

1. The _____ of baking bread involves many steps.

2. The bear _____ the trap, but then he walked away.

3. He _____ around after the party was over.

3 Write the parts for each word.

1. refocused   = _____ + _____ + _____

2. unapproachable = _____ + _____ + _____

3. calmness   = _____ + _____

4. unlimited   = _____ + _____ + _____

1

1. What was the dop machine antenna made from?

_____

2. What does the expression "bum rap" mean?

_____

_____

3. Why did Eddie hope that the telephone call was being tapped?

_____

_____

4. How did Agnes know the truth about Eddie—from his conversation or from his thoughts?

_____

5. Who was the man that Eddie called?

_____

6. Did Eddie trust the man he called? _____

7. How did Agnes set up the dop machine to awaken her during the night?

_____

_____

8. How did Agnes know where the jewels were hidden?

_____

_____

9. Why was Agnes going to have trouble locating the jewels?

_____

_____

10. Write another good title for this story.

_____

2 **Fill in each blank using a word in the box.**

fidgeted	momentary	acquainted
linger	adjustment	superb

1. The nervous boy _____ with his watch.

2. She was afraid for a second, but her fear was only _____.

3. You are not _____ with my Uncle Fernando, are you?

1

1. How did Agnes know what time it was when she arrived at the Rialto Theater?

   _____

   _____

2. Why couldn't the usher immediately tell Agnes where to find a dry cleaning shop?

   _____

3. How did Agnes feel about lying?

   _____

4. What did the sign that interested Agnes say?

   _____

5. Why did the woman at the cleaners need the number of the bag?

   _____

   _____

6. What did Agnes have to do to come up with the number?

   _____

   _____

7. Describe the bag in which the jewel box was hidden.

   _____

   _____

8. Why couldn't Agnes describe the clothes in the bag?

   _____

9. What could Agnes see at the bottom of the cleaning bag?

   _____

10. How do you think Agnes will answer the question at the end of this story?

_____

_____

2 Fill in each blank using a word in the box.

| abruptly | scrawled | rehearsed |
| mission | bulge | momentary |

1. She _____ the song until she got it right.

2. Hiro felt that it was his _____ to help the starving people.

3. Bernice stopped so _____ that change flew out of her pockets.

1

1. What is lava? _____

2. What is a volcano?

   _____

   _____

3. What is the first stage of a volcano called? _____

4. Where did the volcanic eruptions of 1815 and 1883 take place?

   _____

5. What is the volcanic eruption of 1883 compared with?

   _____

   _____

6. How far away could the 1883 volcanic eruption be heard?

   _____

7. What causes an earthquake?

   _____

8. What makes a mountainous coastal area unstable?

   _____

   _____

9. What part of the United States is most liable to experience serious earthquakes?

   _____

10. About how many earthquakes a year do any damage? _____

2 **Fill in each blank using a word in the box.**

acquainted	lava	erupted
lingered	bulge	coastal

1. The _____ was too hot to touch.

2. The smoke from the forest fire _____ in the air for days.

3. Earthquakes frequently occur in _____ areas where mountains rise next to deep seas.

3 **Write the parts for each word.**

1. unsuspecting = _____ + _____ + _____

2. destructiveness = _____ + _____

3. dismissed = _____ + _____ + _____

4. obviously = _____ + _____

1

1. Why did the woman ask Agnes to tell her what was in the bag?

_____

_____

2. What did Agnes say was in the bag?

_____

3. Did the woman believe the jewels were imitation? _____

4. a. Who did Agnes meet as she left the dry cleaning shop?

_____

b. Why had the man come to the dry cleaning shop?

_____

5. Why did Agnes keep glancing back as she walked away from the dry cleaning shop?

_____

6. How did Agnes happen to step right in front of a car?

_____

_____

7. After she'd been running for a while, how did her arms and legs feel?

_____

8. When she couldn't run anymore, what did she try to do?

_____

9. Where was Agnes at the end of this story?

_____

_____

2 **Fill in each blank using a word in the box.**

confidential	imitation	sensed
conveyed	determination	coastal

1. Even though Helen had fallen fourteen times, she still had the

   _____ to keep skating.

2. The frightened horses _____ that wolves were nearby.

3. Joel gave his boss a _____ message.

1

1. How did Agnes escape from the hulk in the office building?

_____

_____

2. Why did Agnes feel safe in the library?

_____

3. Where did Agnes put the jewels?

_____

_____

4. What does "lapidary" mean?

_____

5. Why did Agnes cover her face as she came out of the library?

_____

6. Who was waiting at the bottom of the steps? _____

7. When did Agnes finally feel really safe?

_____

8. Why did Agnes recognize Officer MacCarthy's voice?

_____

_____

9. How did Agnes offer to help when she called the police station?

_____

_____

10. Why did Agnes hang up on Officer MacCarthy?

_____

2 **Fill in each blank using a word in the box.**

familiar	precious	descended
echoing	volume	illegal

1. The robber did many things that were _____.

2. The treasure chest was full of _____ coins and jewels.

3. He wore the same _____ outfit every day.

1

1. Why did Agnes rig up a telephone line to the main cable?

   _____

2. What was Officer MacCarthy thinking when Agnes read his thoughts?

   _____

   _____

3. Where was Officer MacCarthy supposed to find the evidence?

   _____

   _____

4. Why did Officer MacCarthy quickly recognize Ramsey the Crusher from Agnes's

   description? _____

   _____

5. What did Agnes call her unusual powers? _____

6. What deal did Agnes make with the police?

   _____

   _____

   _____

7. What did Agnes tell the police to call her? _____

8. During her first six months as a detective, what did Agnes accomplish?

   _____

   _____

   _____

9. Why did Agnes decide not to turn the dop machine over to the police?

_____

_____

10. According to Agnes's will, what will happen to the dop machine when she dies?

_____

2 **Fill in each blank using a word in the box.**

precious	respected	guaranteed
futile	retrieved	illegal

1. The boys _____ the lunches they had left in the car.

2. The police _____ that the thieves would be caught.

3. Laura made a _____ attempt to catch the faster runner.

3 **Write the parts for each word.**

1. attractiveness = _____ + _____

2. reordering = _____ + _____ + _____

3. untouchable = _____ + _____ + _____

4. disrespect = _____ + _____

1

1. What are the nerves leading from the brain to the body called?

_____

2. How does a reptile brain compare in size and weight to a mammal brain?

_____

_____

3. Why won't a lizard ever adjust if its eyes are rotated?

_____

4. Why did the early mammals become nocturnal?

_____

_____

5. How did early mammals adjust to the darkness?

_____

6. Why did the brain of the early mammal have to change?

_____

_____

7. How might an early mammal have concluded that there was a bird ahead of it?

_____

_____

8. When mammals changed into daylight animals again, how did their eyes work?

_____

_____

9. Why did the night existence of early mammals set the stage for them to become

very intelligent? _____

_____

_____

10. Why did the mammal need a brain that could combine information from various

sense organs? _____

_____

_____

2 **Fill in each blank using a word in the box.**

adjustment	modeled	combined
impressions	futile	retrieve

1. She _____ flour and water in a bowl.

2. The kittens watched as their mother _____ the right way to stalk mice.

3. The mechanic made a small _____ on the motor.

1

1. What are dreams? _____

_____

2. Very little was known about dreams until _____.

3. How long have people had theories and beliefs about dreams?

_____

4. What did the ancient Egyptians believe about dreams?

_____

5. What was one ancient belief about dreams and the soul?

_____

_____

_____

6. What did the dream books of the 1800s say that a dream about falling meant?

_____

7. What do many scientists today think about dreams?

_____

_____

_____

8. What does REM stand for? _____

9. What are some signs that a person is dreaming?

_____

_____

10. How may dreams help keep us emotionally healthy?

_____

_____

_____

2 **Fill in each blank using a word in the box.**

theory	rejected	interpret
symbol	nonsense	represented

1. This is a _____ for a heart: ♡.

2. Lena had a _____ about why Shelton was acting so strangely.

3. The stray dog begged at every doorstep, but the people _____ the dog.

1

1. Where were great reptiles found when they ruled the earth?

_____

2. What is the largest land mammal that ever lived? _____

3. Why hasn't the opossum brain changed from the Mesozoic era until now?

_____

4. The brains of which animals changed the most?

_____

5. How did the horse's size change?

_____

6. Why did the horse's brain change?

_____

7. Why did predators need larger, more complicated brains?

_____

_____

_____

8. a. In land mammals that became sea animals, what changed?

_____

   b. What stayed the same?

_____

9. Why does the killer whale have such a large brain?

_____

_____

10. What is the largest animal that is alive today? _____

11. How large is a blue whale at birth?

_____

2 Fill in each blank using a word in the box.

occupied	complicated	beneficial
theory	avoid	theories

1. The robber hid in the alley to _____ the police officers.

2. Two sparrows _____ the birdhouse.

3. Medicine should be _____ to a sick person.

3 Write the parts for each word.

1. inexpressible = _____ + _____ + _____

2. representing = _____ + _____ + _____

3. undeveloped = _____ + _____ + _____

4. featureless = _____ + _____

Errors

1

1. How did Joe talk his parents into letting him do things?

_____

_____

2. Why did Joe's father agree to let him take the car?

_____

_____

3. How much money would Pete's idea save Joe's father?

_____

4. What was Joe's father supposed to do after putting the valve oil in the engine?

_____

5. How did both Joe and his father end up happy?

_____

_____

6. How did Joe convince a woman customer to buy a toaster?

_____

_____

7. How did the store job limit Joe's talent for selling?

_____

_____

8. Who was Joe going to sell soap to?

_____

9. What did Joe know he would have to do if he was going to succeed in his new job?

_____

2 **Fill in each blank using a word in the box.**

consumer	campaign	demonstrate
manufacture	message	commission

1. Workers _____ tires in a tire factory.

2. Shelly gave many speeches in her _____ to become mayor of the city.

3. For every vacuum cleaner Sam sold, he earned a _____ of $36.

1

1. Who did Joe invite to his party? _____

_____

2. Who were the "hired guests" at the party?

_____

3. How many buyers came?

_____

4. Where was the party held? _____

5. Why did Joe have the party?

_____

6. Where did Joe stand to conduct the auction?

_____

7. How much was each carload of soap worth? _____

8. Why do you think the first carload went for five dollars?

_____

_____

9. How much did the buyer of carload two save his company? _____

10. Why would customers buy "more than soap" once they came into the supermarket?

_____

_____

_____

2 Fill in each blank using a word in the box.

motive	invoice	auction
gimmick	receipt	valves

1. At an _____, people bid on items.

2. A reason to do something is a _____ for doing something.

3. Wardell showed his _____ to prove that he had bought the fan.

1

1. How had the buyers made a good deal on the carloads of Senso soap?

_____

_____

2. Why did Joe have an edge on all the other salespeople after the auction?

_____

_____

_____

3. How did Senso soap sales change in one year?

_____

_____

4. Why didn't Joe want to sell soap for the rest of his life?

_____

_____

5. Why do you think the advertising executive called Joe?

_____

_____

6. What was the problem with the Niota advertising budget?

_____

7. What deal did the advertising agency offer Joe?

_____

_____

8. Why do you think Joe accepted the deal?

_____

_____

9. Who was Joe going to consult after the deal? _____

10. Why did Joe want a Niota to drive?

_____

_____

2 **Fill in each blank using a word in the box.**

| average | challenge | reputation |
| proposition | concluded | executive |

1. A person of _____ height isn't tall and isn't short.

2. Because Elsa wouldn't speak to Ramon, he _____ that she was angry.

3. The _____ did a good job of running his company.

3 **Write the parts for each word.**

1. disability = _____ + _____

2. exclaimed = _____ + _____ + _____

3. unfavorable = _____ + _____ + _____

4. hopelessness = _____ + _____ + _____

Lesson 105

1

1. What legendary figure may have used hypnosis to lure away a group of children?

   _____

2. Who invented the technique called mesmerism?

   _____

3. When people first began to investigate hypnosis, what did they think the trance was

   caused by? _____

4. What did people under hypnosis cling to in order to cure themselves of illness?

   _____

5. You are living in the nineteenth century, and a hypnotist is visiting your town. Describe two things the hypnotist will probably do when you see the performance.

   _____

   _____

6. How was hypnosis used in surgery?

   _____

7. How was hypnosis used in psychiatry?

   _____

8. What famous psychiatrist used hypnosis? _____

9. What does a hypnotized person's behavior depend on?

   _____

   _____

10. How many degrees of hypnosis has one investigator found? _____

2 **Fill in each blank using a word in the box.**

feat	expectations	rigid
anesthetic	extract	conclude

1. On Christmas morning, she had _____ of wonderful presents.

2. Her foot hurt so much that they gave her an _____.

3. He pulled and pulled, but he couldn't _____ the sword from the stone.

1

1. According to Joe's contract with the advertising agency, how was he to be paid?

_____

_____

2. What did Joe have the garage mechanic do? _____

_____

3. How long after he signed the contract did Joe come up with a plan?

_____

4. What does the creative department of an advertising agency do?

_____

5. What does the marketing department of an advertising agency do?

_____

_____

6. How did the president of the agency react to the beginning of Joe's presentation?

_____

_____

7. Why couldn't the Niota compete with the Rondo?

_____

_____

8. What was Joe's plan?

_____

9. How would the other manufacturers help to advertise Car?

_____

_____

10. At the end of this story, was the president convinced that Joe's plan would work?

_____

2 **Fill in each blank using a word in the box.**

contract	media	convince
mechanic	grumbling	inexpensive

1. Radio and television are two forms of _____.

2. Teresa took her car to a _____ to get it fixed.

3. An _____ meal doesn't cost much.

3 **Copy the sentence that tells the main idea of the story.**
   1. The president of the advertising agency did not like the name Joe came up with.
   2. The Niota's engine was not as good as the Rondo's, and the Niota was more expensive.
   3. Joe had a mechanic take the Niota model of car apart and put it back together.
   4. After Joe studied the Niota model of car, he came up with the idea of naming the Niota "Car."

_____

_____

Lesson 107

1

1. What was Joe's plan?

_____

2. Why had the lawyers checked on the name "Car"?

_____

_____

3. How would Car get free advertising?

_____

_____

4. What name did Joe give to the cheapest line of Car? _____

5. a. What word on the billboard was made very small? _____

   b. Why was that word made so small?

   _____

   _____

6. What names did Joe give to the other two lines of Car?

_____

_____

7. How long was the advertising campaign to last? _____

8. How do you know the TV commercials were successful?

_____

_____

9. What did Joe offer the angry dealer who called?

_____

2 **Fill in each blank using a word in the box.**

century	convince	frantic
commercial	imports	budget

1. The company _____ peacock feathers from India.

2. This _____ advertises shaving cream.

3. A hundred years is one _____.

3 **Write the parts for each word.**

1. marvelously   = _____ + _____

2. unfortunately = _____ + _____ + _____

3. extractable   = _____ + _____ + _____

4. worthlessness = _____ + _____ + _____

1. What was the advertising budget for Car?

_____

2. How long did the advertising campaign last? _____

3. Why were the Car dealers angry?

_____

_____

4. What did the president of the advertising agency have to do almost every day?

_____

5. How could the Car campaign hurt other auto dealers?

_____

_____

6. Why did the president of the agency tell reporters that the campaign was a group effort?

_____

_____

7. Why didn't Joe get angry when the president didn't give him credit for the campaign?

_____

_____

8. Why did the labor union protest the Car slogan?

_____

_____

9. Why did the railroad car manufacturer consider a lawsuit against the makers of Car?

_____

_____

10. What words does the story use to describe the weeks that followed the launching of the

Car campaign? _____

2 **Fill in each blank using a word in the box.**

hectic	prior	talent
exhausted	legal	violate

1. Debbie had a _____ for tap dancing.

2. A bird must hatch _____ to learning how to fly.

3. When the supply of pencils was _____, the pencils were all gone.

1

1. What problem did the advertising people have when they talked to the
   Niota executives?

   _____

   _____

2. Why were the Niota executives concerned about Car production?

   _____

   _____

   _____

3. Why could Miyada produce Niotas easily?

   _____

   _____

4. How did the two executives reply to Joe's suggestion about using Miyada?

   _____

   _____

5. Why did Joe think they could get twenty thousand Cars from France?

   _____

6. How much profit would Niota make on the Cars produced by Miyada?

   _____

7. How many Cars would Miyada need to produce for the first year alone?

   _____

8. How many Cars did the agency executives expect would be sold that year
   in their country?

   _____

9. During the meeting with the Niota executives, what did Joe begin to think?

_____

_____

10. What do you think Joe will do about the situation?

_____

_____

2 **Fill in each blank using a word in the box.**

devoted	translated	facilities
launch	thorough	colleagues

1. Pierre _____ a poem from French into English.

2. Your _____ are the people that you work with.

3. Miguel _____ his attention to his homework.

1

1. Why do jet planes fly high above Earth?

_____

_____

2. Is the temperature outside a high-flying jet plane hot or cold? _____

3. Where was the lowest atmospheric temperature ever measured recorded?

_____

4. Where was the record low on Earth's surface recorded?

_____

5. Describe the temperature in Death Valley, California.

_____

6. Where and when was the all-time high temperature reading recorded?

_____

7. What happened to the temperature in Montana in January 1916?

_____

_____

8. What country has the hottest weather year after year? _____

9. How high a building would one hundred feet of snow cover?

_____

10. How long would it take for 366 inches of rain to fall on Chicago or New York?

_____

2 Fill in each blank using a word in the box.

extreme	annually	launch
devote	endured	profit

1. Luisa _____ her hunger until lunchtime.

2. Your birthday is something that happens _____.

3. They selected the plan that was most _____.

3 Write the parts for each word.

1. annually = _____ + _____

2. unbeatable = _____ + _____ + _____

3. substance = _____ + _____

4. dispatch = _____ + _____

1

1. Who found out that Joe had been the brains behind the Car campaign?

   _____

2. What was the title of the reporter's story?

   _____

3. What had Car sales done to sales of domestic cars?

   _____

4. What trick had Joe used to make Car the second-largest-selling import?

   _____

   _____

5. How was the model named "Number One in the Nation" really selling?

   _____

   _____

   _____

6. How had Joe felt about his job before he read the article?

   _____

   _____

7. What did the *Moment* article suggest about Joe's method of selling?

   _____

   _____

8. After reading the *Moment* article, how did Joe spend a lot of his time?

   _____

9. What made Joe decide to fix the situation?

_____

_____

10. What was Joe's new challenge?

_____

_____

2 Fill in each blank using a word in the box.

domestic	intent	devote
genius	deceit	extreme

1. A liar is someone who practices _____.

2. The robber's _____ was to climb up the ladder and go through the window.

3. A very talented person can be called a _____.

1

1. When Joe was thinking about the Niota problem, where did he spend most of the

   afternoon? _____

2. Why did Joe want to meet with the advertising agency executives right away?

   _____

   _____

3. What three facts did Joe use to argue against the Car campaign?

   a. _____

   b. _____

   c. _____

4. What fact did the agency president use to argue against Joe?

   _____

   _____

   _____

5. What point was Joe trying to make when he compared Niota to a duck?

   _____

   _____

   _____

6. Why didn't Joe think they needed the old campaign anymore?

   _____

   _____

7. What new name did Joe propose for Car? _____

8. What kind of "right" did Joe want to sell to car manufacturers?

_____

_____

9. Why did the president of the agency object to Joe's proposal?

_____

_____

10. The head of the marketing department agreed with Joe about something. What?

_____

_____

2 **Fill in each blank using a word in the box.**

bellows	scheduled	strolling
conference	receptionist	resignation

1. The businessman _____ his meeting for two o'clock.

2. When he gets mad, he really _____.

3. Maria wanted to quit, so she handed in her _____.

1

1. How much money did the agency owe Joe?

_____

2. What did Joe threaten to do with his money?

_____

_____

3. Why did Joe think he could sell the agency president on his plan?

_____

4. What was the first step of Joe's new plan?

_____

_____

5. What change would have to be made in the signs at the Car dealerships?

_____

6. Why do you think Joe wanted a lot of reporters there when his plan was announced?

_____

_____

7. How much would Niota charge other car manufacturers for the right to use the word "car"?

_____

8. What would Niota do with that money?

_____

9. How many automobile companies agreed to the terms? _____

10. What happened to the sales of Car after the announcement?

_____

2 Fill in each blank using a word in the box.

withdraw	stroll	rowdies
conference	terms	bellow

1. The _____ jumped and yelled during the meeting.

2. They agreed on the _____ of the contract.

3. Alexia was quick to _____ her hand from the hot stove.

3 Write the parts for each word.

1. preserve   = _____ + _____

2. resigned   = _____ + _____ + _____

3. seriousness   = _____ + _____

4. uninterrupted = _____ + _____ + _____

1

1. What does the word "medicine" in this story refer to?

_____

2. Why did so many of the people who entered a hospital in 1850 die there?

_____

_____

3. What was the cause of the bad smell in a city of 1350?

_____

4. Why were people dirty?

_____

5. Why was the city surrounded by a large wall?

_____

_____

6. What interesting contrast existed in the city?

_____

_____

_____

7. What was the greatest single killer in the city? _____

8. What other diseases were dangerous?

_____

9. Why did most people have scars on their faces?

_____

10. Why do you think the story ends with the sentence, "Perhaps you will regret this

decision"? _____

_____

_____

2 **Fill in each blank using a word in the box.**

treatment	organisms	terms
infected	withdraw	microscope

1. Cats, people, and snakes are all _____.

2. Kamala observed the pin through a _____.

3. Myron was _____ with a cold germ.

1

1. In the earliest picture language, what did each picture stand for?

   _____

2. Later, what did the pictures represent? _____

3. What people developed hieroglyphics?

   _____

4. What are hieroglyphics?

   _____

5. Which came first, spoken language or written language?

   _____

6. How many languages are spoken in the world today? _____

7. In what country are about 140 languages spoken? _____

8. What language is spoken by the greatest number of people?

   _____

9. How many words does the average English-speaking person use?

   _____

10. What is pneumonoultramicroscopicsilicovolcanoconiosis?

    _____

    _____

2 **Fill in each blank using a word in the box.**

treatment	inscribed	determine
infected	withdraw	microscope

1. She _____ "happy birthday" inside the card.

2. Dawn decided to _____ from the contest to be elected
   district attorney.

3. The _____ cured Shoji's cold.

1. What did a black cloth hanging on a house indicate?

_____

_____

2. Why did the doctor use a wand to touch the patient?

_____

_____

3. How did the doctor say he would treat the patient?

_____

4. What did the doctor think caused the Black Death?

_____

_____

5. Why did the doctor say not to bathe the patient?

_____

_____

6. What did the doctor say the smoke would do?

_____

_____

7. What three words of advice did the doctor have for the rich man?

_____

8. Which people were able to escape the plague?

_____

9. How many of the people who remain will become plague victims?

_____

10. How will the doctor die?

_____

2   **Fill in each blank using a word in the box.**

unconscious	tombs	sprinkling
inscribed	impure	treatment

1. Maya was _____ the lawn with a hose.

2. When you are sleeping, you are _____.

3. The muddy water was _____.

3   **Write the parts for each word.**

1. untreatable = _____ + _____ + _____

2. disinfected = _____ + _____ + _____

3. remarkable = _____ + _____ + _____

4. submerge = _____ + _____

Errors

1

1. Name the three types of doctors who worked in 1500.

   a. _____

   b. _____

   c. _____

2. Why did surgeons of the long robe "bleed" patients?

   _____

   _____

3. What kind of work did physicians do?

   _____

   _____

4. What language did physicians and surgeons speak and read? _____

5. What kind of work was done in a "barber shop"?

   _____

   _____

6. Why was it a crime for doctors to study dead bodies?

   _____

   _____

7. What does "anatomy" mean?

   _____

8. a. How did doctors study anatomy?

_____

b. Why didn't this method help to find out facts about the human body?

_____

_____

9. What did Leonardo and Paré seek? _____

2 **Fill in each blank using a word in the box.**

wounds	amputate	sluggish
purify	ignorant	scalding

1. You are _____ of something that you do not know.

2. Barb felt slow and _____ in the mornings.

3. After I _____ the water, the germs will all be dead.

Errors

1

1. How did Leonardo learn so much about human anatomy?

_____

2. What had Leonard hoped to publish?

_____

3. Name two other things that Leonardo accomplished.

_____

_____

_____

4. How did Paré begin his work in medicine?

_____

5. What were the two things that battlefield surgeons could do for wounded soldiers?

_____

6. What slogan did army surgeons use when treating wounds?

_____

_____

7. What two changes did Paré make in treating wounds?

a. _____

_____

b. _____

_____

8. How did these two changes help wounded soldiers?

_____

_____

9. Why did many doctors not respect Paré?

_____

_____

_____

10. What did Paré do to help women?

_____

_____

_____

2 Fill in each blank using a word in the box.

sketches	selection	ignorant
dressing	anatomy	masterpiece

1. The artist drew quick _____ of the model.

2. She wrapped his wound in a clean _____.

3. A class in _____ studies the human body.

1

1. Why did it take courage to question established theories in 1500?

   _____

   _____

2. In 1500, how long had the basic theories of medicine been established?

   _____

3. Who developed the theory of medicine accepted in 1500? _____

4. What does the study of anatomy deal with?

   _____

5. Why couldn't Galen study the structure of the human body?

   _____

   _____

6. How did Galen try to understand human anatomy?

   _____

7. From what animal did Galen get his ideas about the structure of human hipbones?

   _____

8. Why did Galen have mistaken ideas about human anatomy?

   _____

   _____

9. Who were three people who challenged medical theories accepted in 1500?

   _____

10. What traits did Vesalius and Paré have in common?

    _____

    _____

    _____

2 Fill in each blank using a word in the box.

suspicious	selection	elaborate
proclaimed	limbs	masterpiece

1. "I am the best in the west," he _____.

2. A guard dog will be _____ of strangers.

3. Something that is _____ is complicated.

3 Write the parts for each word.

1. unintelligently = _____ + _____ + _____

2. reinfected = _____ + _____ + _____

3. uninhabited = _____ + _____ + _____

4. dissecting = _____ + _____ + _____

1

1. What is the brain composed of? _____

2. What does the story compare nerve cells with?

   _____

   _____

3. How many nerve cells are in the brain? _____

4. What is the corpus callosum?

   _____

   _____

5. What are the two halves of the brain called? _____

6. What is the simple rule for describing what the two hemispheres of the brain do?

   _____

   _____

7. If you can't speak or understand what others are saying, what has probably happened to your brain?

   _____

8. Write **L** if the left hemisphere controls the behavior or **R** if the right hemisphere controls the behavior.

   _____ a. language   _____ c. feel emotion

   _____ b. logical reasoning _____ d. listen to a melody

9. What is a lesion? _____

10. How can a tremor sometimes be eliminated?

    _____

    _____

2 **Fill in each blank using a word in the box.**

composed	elaborate	eliminate
functions	proclaimed	logical

1. Holding things is one of the _____ that your hands perform.

2. A _____ theory makes sense.

3. A car is _____ of many metal parts.

Errors

1

1. What was the dangerous thing Vesalius did in order to study human anatomy?

_____

_____

2. What did he discover from studying the skeleton?

_____

_____

3. What position did Vesalius accept at the age of twenty-three?

_____

4. Give an example of what Vesalius discovered while working there.

_____

_____

5. How did Vesalius prepare to publish his work?

_____

_____

6. Why did the doctors react as they did to Vesalius's book?

_____

_____

_____

7. How did Vesalius explain the difference between his observations and Galen's?

_____

_____

8. What did Vesalius become after leaving the university?

_____

9. How did Vesalius die?

_____

_____

10. What do you think Vesalius accomplished by his work?

_____

_____

2 **Fill in each blank using a word in the box.**

gallows	cautiously	liver
criminal	internal	composed

1. The fox snuck _____ into the chicken yard.

2. The criminal was hanged on the _____.

3. An _____ injury is an injury inside your body.

Errors

1

1. Why was life expectancy in the cities only about thirty-seven years in 1850?

_____

2. What is blood poisoning?

_____

_____

3. What causes blood poisoning? _____

4. Why were people afraid to be vaccinated?

_____

_____

_____

5. Before Pasteur's work, where did most people think flies and other small life-forms

came from? _____

6. Why were some doctors slow to believe that bacteria existed? _____

_____

7. How is milk made safe to drink? _____

8. How do germs cause disease?

_____

9. What did Semmelweis observe about deaths of women in his hospital?

_____

_____

10. Who were the staff in Division One of the hospital?

_____

2 **Fill in each blank using a word in the box.**

bacteria	explanation	internal
vaccination	substance	gallows

1. Gum is a sticky _____.

2. _____ cause some diseases.

3. After the teacher's _____, the students understood how engines work.

3 **Write the parts for each word.**

1. unexpected   = _____ + _____ + _____

2. subdivision   = _____ + _____

3. unacceptable = _____ + _____ + _____

4. rearrange   = _____ + _____

1

1. What problem was Semmelweis concerned with?

   _____

   _____

2. What were six explanations of this problem that Semmelweis rejected?

   a. _____

   b. _____

   c. _____

   d. _____

   e. _____

   f. _____

3. When a doctor died of a fever similar to childbed fever, what did Semmelweis assume?

   _____

   _____

4. What did doctors and students do that nurses did not do?

   _____

5. What two changes did Semmelweis introduce that greatly reduced the death rate in Division One?

   a. _____

   _____

   b. _____

   _____

6. What effect did these changes have? _____

_____

7. What was the reaction of the medical profession to Semmelweis's procedures?

_____

_____

8. What disease did Semmelweis die of?

_____

9. Why is Semmelweis considered a great man?

_____

_____

10. What is the basic principle that Semmelweis introduced?

_____

_____

2 Fill in each blank using a word in the box.

punctured	diet	resisted
hostility	frequently	stale

1. A place I visit _____ is the theater on Main Street.

2. The food got _____ from sitting in the cupboard.

3. She _____ by not letting her sister take the comic book.

1. Name three things doctors in 1900 knew about that doctors in 1500 did not know about.

   a. _____

   b. _____

   c. _____

2. What is one terrible disease that doctors have learned to cure in the last 100 years?

   _____

3. Name a drug that doctors use to control infections.

   _____

4. What is a midwife?

   _____

   _____

5. Why were there no women doctors a little over one hundred years ago?

   _____

   _____

6. Who was the first woman to receive a medical degree?

   _____

7. In what year did she receive her degree? _____

8. How has the role of women in medicine changed?

   _____

9. Why do most doctors specialize?

   _____

   _____

10. In what way were Paré, Vesalius, and the others you've read about brave?

_____

_____

_____

2 **Fill in each blank using a word in the box.**

penicillin	puncture	attitude
resistance	symptoms	hostility

1. Bob's cough was one of the _____ of his cold.

2. The dog's _____ toward cats was that they should be chased.

3. The harmful bacteria were killed by the _____ that she took.

3 **Write the parts for each word.**

1. carelessness = _____ + _____ + _____

2. redesigned = _____ + _____ + _____

3. unpunishable = _____ + _____ + _____

4. replaceable = _____ + _____ + _____

1

1. What is a funambulist?

   _____

2. Where did Charles Blondin perform an incredible walk?

   _____

3. How long was the rope Blondin used for his walk? _____

4. The country Charles Blondin was from is:

   ○ England   ○ United States   ○ France   ○ Canada

5. Why did Blondin's agent become ill after Blondin carried him on the tightrope?

   _____

   _____

6. When was the record set for the longest tightrope walk?

   ○ 1885   ○ 1974   ○ 2005   ○ 1969

7. How far did Rochetain walk when he crossed from one side of a gorge to another?

   _____

8. How long did it take Rochetain to make that walk?

   _____

9. What is the endurance record for being on a tightrope?

   ○ 310 days   ○ 205 days   ○ 110 days   ○ 185 days

10. What puzzled doctors about Rochetain's record stay on a tightrope?

    ○ Food was delivered to him on the wire.

    ○ He walked along the rope to stay in condition.

    ○ He was able to sleep while balanced on the wire.

    ○ He never left the wire for any reason.

2 Fill in each blank using a word in the box.

disappointing	obviously	endurance
secured	designed	casually

1. The funambulist Blondin walked _____ along the tightrope high above the river.

2. The workers _____ the circus tent by tying ropes to several metal stakes.

3. Carla set the _____ record for standing on one foot longer than anyone else in her class.

3 Write the parts for each word.

1. disappointed = _____ + _____ + _____

2. impressive = _____ + _____ + _____

3. unfortunately = _____ + _____ + _____

4. transplanted = _____ + _____ + _____

5. shipwrecked = _____ + _____ + _____

Name: _____   Date: _____

1

	A	B	C	D
1.	○ gaunt	○ gain	○ giant	○ gent
2.	○ chance	○ changes	○ charges	○ chances
3.	○ bonding	○ bending	○ bounding	○ bouncing
4.	○ try	○ tried	○ tied	○ tired
5.	○ swilled	○ swerved	○ swelled	○ swirled
6.	○ from	○ front	○ form	○ frown
7.	○ pointed	○ painted	○ pounded	○ pouted
8.	○ ducked	○ docked	○ dock	○ duck
9.	○ poked	○ packed	○ pokes	○ poke
10.	○ strained	○ stained	○ sprained	○ sprain
11.	○ started	○ startled	○ stared	○ stirred
12.	○ which	○ wish	○ watch	○ wash
13.	○ through	○ thought	○ tough	○ though
14.	○ spare	○ spar	○ spray	○ stare
15.	○ every	○ even	○ very	○ ever
16.	○ steep	○ stripe	○ strip	○ street

	A	B	C	D
17.	○ quit	○ quiet	○ quick	○ quite
18.	○ slime	○ slim	○ slam	○ smile
19.	○ fender	○ flounder	○ founder	○ fonder
20.	○ trump	○ tuck	○ truck	○ trunk
21.	○ expert	○ expect	○ explain	○ extinct
22.	○ listening	○ listing	○ listed	○ listener
23.	○ fist	○ first	○ fierce	○ farce
24.	○ rear	○ roar	○ rare	○ road
25.	○ boat	○ beast	○ based	○ boast

Part 1

Number of errors [   ]

25 items

2

	A	B	C	D
1.	○ cautioned	○ continental	○ continual	○ intentional
2.	○ extensive	○ expecting	○ pretender	○ expensive
3.	○ conditioner	○ cautioned	○ vaccinate	○ continent
4.	○ apartment	○ desperate	○ contraption	○ reporter
5.	○ external	○ retorted	○ entirely	○ retarded

Part 2

Number of errors [   ]

5 items

3

Trapped in the Storm

"We're in for it now," Doris exclaimed.

"What are we going to do?" Jane asked. "Those waves are going to hit us in a few minutes."

The women swam back to their boat, towing the spare air tank. They climbed aboard. Jane and Doris grabbed the oars and started rowing as fast as they could. After they rowed for nearly half an hour, Jane exclaimed, "I don't know where to go. We've got to find some protection from that storm, but I don't see any protection."

"Let's keep moving along the reef," Doris suggested. "Maybe we can find a place where the reef is high enough to protect the boat."

Jane glanced back. The clouds were closer, and the whitecaps seemed to be bigger and wilder. The old scow continued to move slowly along the west side of the reef. Jane glanced back at the clouds again.

"Look," Doris said. Doris was pointing ahead. "There's an old ship over there." It was a great steamer that had been salvaged over 70 years ago. It was now pinned against the reef.

Jane caught a glimpse of it. The women were about half a mile from the steamer.

"I wish this boat would move faster," Jane shouted. Before Doris could respond, however, a fierce gust of cold wind swept past the boat, making ruffled patterns in the water. The boat turned slightly when the wind hit it.

"Here it comes," Doris shouted. Jane could hardly hear Doris's voice above the wind. Already whitecaps were forming. The wind was blowing the tops of the waves into a fine spray.

Jane licked her lips. They were salty. "Let's raise the sail," Doris said. "The wind will take us to the old ship."

A few moments later, the small sail was up. The wind pushed against it so fiercely that Doris thought the sail would rip apart. But it held, and the boat picked up speed and rolled along with the breakers.

The waves were now starting to roll over the low places along the reef. As the waves rolled under the boat, the boat began to sway from side to side. The swaying, which was gentle at first, became more violent. From time to time one of the waves would splash against the side of the boat and send warm water streaming into the boat. Doris was bailing when the boat was only about three hundred feet from the steamer.

When the old boat was less than a hundred feet from the steamer, the mast collapsed and the sail fluttered as the wind whipped it around violently. "Grab the oars," Doris shouted. "We'll have to row." She stopped bailing and again picked up the oars. The old boat didn't seem to make much headway, but slowly it approached the steamer.

"I don't have much more strength," Jane shouted above the raging wind.

A huge breaker slammed against the side of the boat and turned the boat halfway around. Another wave struck the boat and almost sent Jane overboard. But somehow, Doris managed to keep rowing, and the boat slowly moved behind the steamer. Huge breakers were smashing against the other side of the steamer, sending plumes of spray into the air. But the boat was in a protected place.

4

1. Where did Jane and Doris go to protect the boat?

   _____

2. At first, what did the women do to move toward the protected place?

   ○ ran the engine   ○ sailed   ○ rowed   ○ swam

3. After the wind came up, what did they do to move toward the protected place?

   _____

4. What happened when they were less than a hundred feet from the protected place?

   ○ Their boat sank.   ○ The wind died down.

   ○ The mast broke.   ○ The steamer moved away.

5. Why did Jane almost fall out of the boat?

   ○ The boat ran into the reef.   ○ The boat ran into the steamer.

   ○ A wave hit the steamer.   ○ A wave hit the boat.

6. Which happened first?

   ○ The women saw a protected place.

   ○ The mast broke.

   ○ Doris started bailing.

   ○ The women saw whitecaps and dark clouds.

7. At the end of the selection, where were Doris and Jane?

   ○ In the wind

   ○ Behind the steamer

   ○ On an island

   ○ Behind a coral reef

Part 4

Number of errors [   ]

7 items

Total errors - Test 2

P F

37 items

Name: _____

Date: _____

1

	A	B	C	D
1.	○ motions	○ motionless	○ motiveless	○ motorless
2.	○ experiments	○ expirations	○ experience	○ experiences
3.	○ brothers	○ blotters	○ bothers	○ boaters
4.	○ messenger	○ meandered	○ measurer	○ measured
5.	○ viscosity	○ viciously	○ victoriously	○ vicinity
6.	○ union	○ unicorn	○ unison	○ unicycle
7.	○ released	○ relished	○ release	○ reliance
8.	○ serially	○ certainly	○ seriously	○ subtly
9.	○ indelible	○ incredible	○ identical	○ inconceivable
10.	○ infected	○ inflict	○ inflated	○ inflicted
11.	○ swept	○ steeped	○ seeped	○ seeded
12.	○ winner	○ wonder	○ wander	○ winder
13.	○ diet	○ dried	○ did	○ died
14.	○ lotus	○ locates	○ locusts	○ lucks
15.	○ transferred	○ transformed	○ reformed	○ transient
16.	○ conducted	○ concocted	○ connected	○ contradicted

	A	B	C	D
17.	○ detector	○ dictator	○ director	○ decider
18.	○ physical	○ physiques	○ psychics	○ physics
19.	○ users	○ husher	○ ushers	○ eskers
20.	○ couple	○ capitol	○ capsule	○ copula
21.	○ prominence	○ prominent	○ provident	○ promenade
22.	○ locative	○ locomotion	○ lucrative	○ locomotive
23.	○ pleasant	○ plunger	○ pleasure	○ plumber
24.	○ researches	○ researchers	○ resources	○ reserved
25.	○ prospector	○ professional	○ processional	○ profitable
26.	○ creator	○ crater	○ creature	○ creditor
27.	○ apology	○ apologize	○ energize	○ optimize
28.	○ faster	○ facer	○ faker	○ factor

Part 1

Number of errors [ ]

28 items

A Practical Joke That Failed

One of the worst practical jokes that Milly ever played took place out in the Virginia hills. Milly, Fred, and Fred's wife, Angie, were camping. It was in the early fall. Milly told the others, "Now this time of year, the bears may get a little vicious. If you see a bear, just stand still and the bear probably won't bother you."

"So now you tell us about this," Fred said. "We've been planning this thing for more than a month. During that time, you haven't said one word about bears."

"I'm sorry," Milly said. "It must have slipped my mind."

That statement was not exactly true. Milly had brought along a tape player with an automatic timer. The tape in her player made the most fierce bear roars imaginable. Those roars were so realistic and so terrifying that Milly could hardly keep from laughing every time she played the tape.

And that's just what she planned to do—play that tape, at night, when Fred and Angie went into the woods with Milly on their way to see glowworms.

By sundown, Milly had already placed the tape player in the woods near the path. And she was busy setting up the joke. "There are some amazing glowworms down near the stream." She and Angie were sitting in front of the tent, near the last of the campfire. "I've never seen real glowworms," Angie said. "What do they look like?"

"They are just little worms. But they glow in the dark. And they make little strings that hang down, and guess what? Those strings that glow in the dark? There are hundreds of strings glowing like little electric lights down by the stream."

"Let's go see them," Angie said.

"We can't do it now," Milly responded. "There's too much daylight."

When it was nearly dark, both Fred and Angie accompanied Milly. She stopped in a secluded place a few yards from the tape player.

Milly announced, "You may be able to get a glimpse of the glowworms from here if you look toward the stream, and you certainly will be able to hear their sound. It's very distinctive, like tiny locusts."

As Fred and Angie peered in the direction of the stream, Milly delicately hid behind a tree and stood motionless. "I can't see them or hear them," Fred said.

A moment later, Milly pressed the remote control button, and the silence was shattered by an enormous roar. Angie instinctively scrambled up the path toward the tent, thrashing through the underbrush, but Fred stood incredibly still as if paralyzed. Milly had planned to leap out and scare both of them, but Fred appeared to be so frightened that she took pity on him and started to laugh in her impish way as she stepped from behind the tree.

Fred did not change his expression. His wide eyes seemed to almost shine in the gathering darkness. Milly stopped laughing and said in a remorseful voice, "Oh, I'm sorry, Fred. I didn't mean to . . ."

Fred pointed very slowly and whispered, "Over there. . . ."

Milly turned to see what he was referring to, and when she did, she instinctively let out a little gasp. It was a tremendous bear, standing upright not ten feet from them.

Without realizing what she was doing, she cried out, "Holy cow," and stampeded toward the tent as fast as she could. When she heard Fred and Angie laughing, she slowed down. She was seriously confused.

"Wha . . . what's . . ." she stammered.

Fred strolled up to her and explained, "When you plan one of your jokes you should make sure you don't tell anybody about it—like the guy at the electronics store. We found out about your joke." Both he and Angie started to giggle. "And we're going to have a lot of fun telling everybody how you ran like a scared rabbit from the cardboard bear we set up near your tape player."

1. Where were Milly, Fred, and Angie camping?

   ○ in a campground   ○ in the Colorado hills

   ○ in Virginia   ○ near a large lake

2. What did Milly tell Fred and Angie they should do if they saw a bear?

   ○ run toward the tent   ○ stand motionless

   ○ sing in a soft voice ○ shoot it

3. Why had Milly gone to the electronics store before she went to the woods?

   ○ To get lights for the tent

   ○ To get three electric heaters

   ○ To get a tape player with a remote control device

   ○ To get a tape player without a remote control device

4. Why did Milly say they had to wait until dark before going down the path

   toward the stream?

   ○ Because they could see the bears in the daylight.

   ○ Because they couldn't see glowworms in the daylight.

   ○ Because everybody would see the cardboard bear.

   ○ Because everybody would be able to hear the tape player.

5. Both Fred and Angie <u>accompanied</u> Milly. What does "accompanied" mean?

   ○ frightened   ○ acknowledged

   ○ went with   ○ looked at

6. She stopped in a <u>secluded</u> place. What does "secluded" mean?

   ○ treacherous   ○ dark

   ○ small   ○ hidden

7. Why did Milly run toward the tent?

   ○ Because Angie ran toward the tent.

   ○ Because she saw a cardboard bear.

   ○ Because Fred was laughing at her.

   ○ Because there were glowworms in the path.

8. Why did Milly slow down when she was running toward the tent?

   ○ She was becoming tired.

   ○ She encountered a bear.

   ○ Her tape recorder let out a great roar.

   ○ She heard laughter.

9. Which answer tells about the jokes that were played in this selection?

   ○ Angie's joke and then Milly's joke

   ○ Fred and Angie's joke and then Milly's joke

   ○ Milly's joke and then Fred and Angie's joke

   ○ Fred's joke and then Angie's joke

Part 3

Number of errors [ ]

9 items

Name: _____ Date: _____

1

	A	B	C	D
1.	○ apportion	○ abhorrence	○ apparent	○ appearance
2.	○ discussions	○ discussers	○ discussion	○ decision
3.	○ experimental	○ experiments	○ experiences	○ equipment
4.	○ germination	○ generates	○ gentian	○ generations
5.	○ scarce	○ scare	○ scary	○ sparse
6.	○ possibly	○ possibility	○ potability	○ prosody
7.	○ invincible	○ invisible	○ incredible	○ inevitable
8.	○ apprentice	○ depreciate	○ appreciate	○ approximate
9.	○ mediator	○ moderation	○ moderator	○ modernizer
10.	○ reinvesting	○ revisiting	○ reevaluating	○ reinstating
11.	○ assassinate	○ associates	○ association	○ associate
12.	○ disbelieve	○ debrief	○ disability	○ disbelief
13.	○ abruptly	○ appropriately	○ abroad	○ abrupt
14.	○ sense	○ scene	○ scents	○ scenery
15.	○ phony	○ phones	○ pony	○ fondly
16.	○ indemnify	○ identity	○ ideally	○ identify

	A	B	C	D
17.	○ pursued	○ persisted	○ persuaded	○ purported
18.	○ schemed	○ scheduled	○ skewed	○ schedule
19.	○ coincide	○ coinage	○ coinsurance	○ coincidence
20.	○ accent	○ acidic	○ accident	○ axial
21.	○ pennyweight	○ penetrate	○ pendulum	○ pinnate
22.	○ clammy	○ comely	○ calumny	○ calmly
23.	○ diagnosis	○ dialoguing	○ diagramming	○ diagnosing
24.	○ applause	○ apparent	○ apparatus	○ appearance
25.	○ demonstrates	○ designate	○ denigrate	○ demonstrate
26.	○ transfer	○ transit	○ transmit	○ transmits
27.	○ patient	○ patent	○ potent	○ pittance
28.	○ momentous	○ monetary	○ monastery	○ momentary
29.	○ obvious	○ oblivious	○ objectives	○ obligates
30.	○ usual	○ unused	○ unusual	○ unusable

Part 1

Number of errors ☐

30 items

Roads and Highways

People have had roads for over six thousand years. The early roads were built along trails made by animals. Explorers followed these trails. Roads that used these trails had several problems. One was that the roads would sometimes flood. Another problem was that the roads would get muddy in the spring. Hundreds of years ago, road builders in England started to build "highways." The roads were called "highways" because the builders would make the roads higher than the land around them. In that way, the roads wouldn't flood.

In addition to being higher than the surroundings, the highway was "surfaced." The surface could be any kind of material that would permit the road to be used during wet seasons. Some of the surfaces were rocks, some flat stones, and some bricks. Roman engineers were the first to build really good roads. They used flat stones to make roads that were 50 feet wide. The middle of the road was higher than the side, so that water would drain from the road. The engineers dug ditches next to the road so the water would flow to lower places.

The Romans built over 50,000 miles of stone roads. Their roads went in a straight line. Instead of going around hills, these roads went over the hills. At that time, carts and wagons had wheels. The roads made travel far easier than it would be on a dirt trail.

In the United States, the early roads built in the 1800s were constructed of wooden blocks, bricks, or stones. These roads were built long before there were automobiles.

Roads were called "streets" when they were in cities. Most of the early roads in the United States were streets. People who wanted to travel across country had to use dirt roads. Also, small towns often did not have surfaced roads. Some roads were constructed of logs, which made them very bumpy and required frequent repair.

At the time the California Gold Rush was going on, people could travel long distances in comfort, but not on roads. People could travel on trains. By 1870, it was possible to go across the entire United States on trains. Not much progress occurred on highway construction because traveling by train was faster than walking on roads or riding in a coach pulled by horses.

A bigger problem with the roads was that they were not coordinated, which meant it was not easy to go a long distance. In 1912, there were two and a half million miles of roads, but most were dirt, with no surface. Typically, roads would wander from a community, but most roads did not connect to other roads. They would lead to a farm, and usually there were no street or road signs to tell where the road went. Travelers not familiar with the area would often go back to the last community and ask somebody which combination of roads would get them to the next community.

When the early automobiles were built, a lot of people thought they would never become popular because they didn't go any faster than a bicycle. They were also expensive, they were not reliable, and it was difficult to get fuel for them.

Henry Ford was the inventor who was responsible for changing transportation in the world. He didn't invent the car; he invented ways to mass-produce cars so they would cost far less than earlier cars. He also built them so they could go almost anywhere in the country. His goal was to build vehicles—cars and tractors—that farmers could use. Ford's most famous car was the Model T. It had very high ground clearance, which meant that it could go over hills and through gullies that most modern cars could not handle without getting stuck.

But even the Model T Ford was not always reliable. During wet periods, the Model T would make two grooves in the road, one created by the left tires and the other by the right tires. Every time the car went down the road, the grooves would get deeper until they were so deep that even the Model T got stuck.

In 1913, several businessmen had an idea that would make long-distance travel by automobile far simpler. They would construct a coast-to-coast rock highway that would go from New York City to San Francisco. This highway was to have a hard surface made of crushed rock in some places and concrete in others. The businessmen who were responsible for the road named it the Lincoln Highway to honor Abraham Lincoln. Work began on the Lincoln Highway in 1913, but progress was slow. By 1916, a traveler could go all the way across the United States on the Lincoln Highway, but the road was not completed. In parts, it was not surfaced.

The Lincoln Highway was not the only main road in the United States. By 1925 there were about 250 major routes. All these roads had names, but they were not coordinated. Often, these routes did not have signs that told travelers the name of the road. The only information about a route was colored bands on telephone poles. Sometimes, more than one route would use parts of the same road, and there could be ten or more bands on a telephone pole.

In 1926, the government decided to coordinate highways and make a national system of highways. As part of this organization, the names were dropped and replaced by numbers. The numbering system had even numbers for highways that went east and west and odd numbers for highways that went north and south. Travelers could now tell whether the road was going in the direction they wanted. The Lincoln Highway went east and west, so it was renamed as U.S. Route 30. Route 1 went north and south.

Some older people still refer to Route 30 as the Lincoln Highway, but other numbered routes are known only as numbers—like Route 66. The number tells what direction that highway goes.

3

1. The earliest roads were built along
   - ○ mountains.
   - ○ streams.
   - ○ ditches.
   - ○ animal trails.

2. Roads were called "highways" when they were
   - ○ dirt roads.
   - ○ raised roads.
   - ○ straight roads.
   - ○ wide roads.

3. Highways were also
   - ○ dirt.
   - ○ rutted.
   - ○ surfaced.
   - ○ muddy.

4. Who built the first system of roads that were surfaced?
   - ○ Americans
   - ○ Greeks
   - ○ British
   - ○ Romans

5. Why were highways built so the middle was higher than the sides?
   - ○ To permit more vehicles on the road
   - ○ To help vehicles travel in a straight line
   - ○ To drain water from the road
   - ○ To make the surface harder

6. Roads in cities were are called
   - ○ cobblestones.
   - ○ paths.
   - ○ highways.
   - ○ streets.

7. Which description tells about roads in the 1800s?
   - ○ All were well coordinated.
   - ○ All were surfaced.
   - ○ They were marked with colored bands.
   - ○ Most were dirt roads.

8. Which is true about the Model T?

   ○ It was costly.

   ○ It was handmade.

   ○ It was made by Henry Ford's company.

   ○ It could not go on rough, dirt roads.

9. Which statement is not true about the Lincoln Highway?

   ○ The highway went from New York to California.

   ○ The highway was marked by colored bands on telephone poles.

   ○ The highway was completed in 1913.

   ○ The highway was named after a president of the United States.

10. Which of the following highways goes north and south?

   ○ Route 66   ○ Route 30

   ○ Route 81   ○ Route 12

Number of errors

Part 3

9 items

Name: _____   Date: _____

1

	A	B	C	D

1. ○ excellent   ○ excelled   ○ excellence   ○ exception

2. ○ presentation   ○ prevention   ○ preparation   ○ perforation

3. ○ transformer   ○ translator   ○ transporter   ○ transactor

4. ○ measures   ○ messages   ○ messengers   ○ mesmerizes

5. ○ antiseptic   ○ anesthetics   ○ anatomic   ○ anesthetic

6. ○ increase   ○ incurable   ○ incredible   ○ incredibly

7. ○ encompass   ○ enclosure   ○ encourage   ○ encounter

8. ○ important   ○ impressed   ○ imported   ○ importance

9. ○ progression   ○ procession   ○ profession   ○ proposition

10. ○ ineffective   ○ inefficient   ○ infantile   ○ infectious

11. ○ securely   ○ seriously   ○ secretly   ○ secretary

12. ○ disguised   ○ discussed   ○ diseased   ○ displeased

13. ○ oration   ○ operation   ○ organization   ○ apparition

14. ○ unconvincingly   ○ unconsciously   ○ uncommonly   ○ uncertainly

15. ○ prevailing   ○ preventing   ○ pertaining   ○ preparing

16. ○ deception   ○ distribution   ○ discussion   ○ dissection

	A	B	C	D
17.	○ parent	○ partner	○ pattern	○ parrots
18.	○ subside	○ substance	○ substitute	○ substantial
19.	○ reception	○ reputation	○ rejection	○ reflection
20.	○ commonly	○ committee	○ company	○ community
21.	○ departed	○ depressed	○ descended	○ depended
22.	○ thrashes	○ trusses	○ trashes	○ thrushes
23.	○ incredible	○ invisible	○ incurable	○ incapable
24.	○ recorded	○ reconstructed	○ resounded	○ recovered
25.	○ reverse	○ revisit	○ research	○ reserve
26.	○ unsteadily	○ uniformity	○ university	○ universally
27.	○ produces	○ procedures	○ proceeds	○ processes
28.	○ stacker	○ stagger	○ slacker	○ slicker
29.	○ appeal	○ appearance	○ apparel	○ apparent
30.	○ invited	○ invoiced	○ invented	○ inverted

Part 1

Number of errors

30 items

Birds and Bats

2

A bird's body has many unusual features. The most remarkable of these is its feathers. A bird depends on its feathers for its flying power.

Reptiles and some mammals, such as squirrels, developed a special kind of wing. This wing consisted of skin that was stretched over the hand bones. The hand bones had gradually become long and slender, and the skin worked like the surface of a kite. Birds developed a similar wing. But birds' wings evolved differently. Their arm and finger bones became long and hollow, but they didn't develop skin over these bones. They developed feathers. Gradually feathers became highly specialized parts of a bird's anatomy.

A feather is made up of a large number of dead cells. These cells consist mostly of air. Therefore, the feather is extremely light. At the center of a feather is a stiff shaft called the quill. The upper part of the quill has barbs on each side. The feather is designed so that when it moves in one direction, no air can pass between the barbs of the feather. But when the feather moves in the other direction, the feather does not grab the air.

The body structure of the bird is highly specialized, just as the wing structure is specialized. This specialization permits swift and powerful flight. If you compare the bird's body with that of a human being, the bird has a shorter trunk (including the chest and waist) area. The bird also has a stiffer backbone and rib cage than a human being. The rib cage is rigid so the bird can maintain its body in a fixed position during flight. What is most striking about the bird's strong body structure is its lightness.

Different species of birds have wings that are well adapted to the bird's purposes for flying—wings for gliding, wings for soaring, wings for maneuvering quickly, and wings for short fast flights. Birds that travel long distances have long wings that move slowly but that have good capacity for gliding.

Because different species of birds have adapted to different environments, many species are unique. The penguin actually swims underwater. Its wings are useless outside the water and are not designed for flight in the air; however, they are perfectly designed to propel penguins quite fast underwater.

One of the most interesting birds is the hummingbird. Actually, there are 320 different species of hummingbirds, each with different habits and different body structures. All hummingbirds are able to hover and even move backward while they are in flight. They use their hovering ability when they feed. They approach a flower with nectar and then fly forward enough to put their pointed beak inside the flower and reach the nectar. After extracting the nectar, they fly backward, turn, and fly to the next flower.

All the body processes of the hummingbird are very fast, compared to those of a human. The human heart rate is about 72 beats per minute, but the hummingbird's heart rate is 1,260 beats per minute, which is 21 beats per second. The rate at which the hummingbird's tongue laps nectar is 13 licks per second. The reason they are called hummingbirds is that they flap their wings so fast they make a whirring, humming sound. To achieve this sound, hummingbirds flap their wings at an amazing rate, 80 times per second.

Because hummingbirds have such fast body processes, they have to eat a great amount of food every day compared to how much they weigh. A full-grown hummingbird weighs about as much as a penny. Four young hummingbirds could fit in a teaspoon. The smallest hummingbird in the world is the bee hummingbird, which lives in Cuba. It is called a bee hummingbird because it is about the size of a large bee, less than two inches long and weighing so little that two adults weigh less than a penny. One of the big dangers for the bee hummingbird is spider webs, because bee hummingbirds don't have enough weight or power to escape from webs.

Birds are not the only warm-blooded animals that fly. Bats are the only mammals capable of true flight. The bat's wings are different from those of birds primarily because they are not covered with feathers. Instead, they are covered with skin. The diagram on the next page shows that the bat wing is an arm with an enlarged hand that has a thumb and four fingers. The thumb bone is tiny, but the others are greatly enlarged. Notice that all bats have five-toed feet.

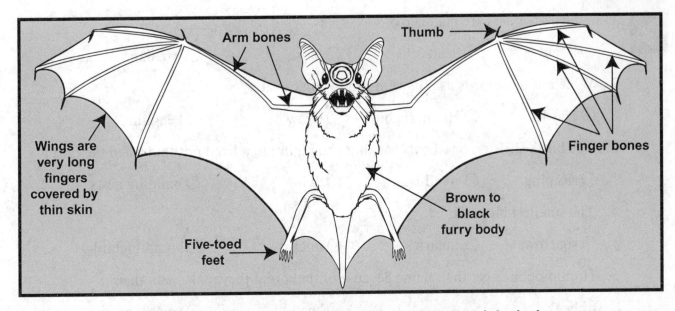

Arm bones

Thumb

Finger bones

Wings are
very long
fingers
covered by
thin skin

Brown to
black
furry body

Five-toed
feet

At one time, a bat was called a "flitter-mouse" because it looked like a mouse. If somebody guessed how many different species of bats there are, the person might guess 8, 10, even 20. Amazingly, there are over 900 different species of bat. These range in size from the bumblebee bat, which is not much bigger than a bumblebee and weighs less than a penny, to the giant vampire bat and foxtail bat, which weigh more than four pounds and may have a wingspan of six feet.

One of the most prevalent myths about bats is that they are blind. All species have functioning eyes. Some species do not see well, but many have keen eyesight and use their eyes when hunting. Bats also use what's called **echolocation** to locate objects at night when many bats hunt for food. Bats send out high-pitched sounds that bounce off objects and create an echo that returns to the bat's ears. The bat's brain figures out where the object is by computing how long it takes for the sound to reach the object and send an echo back to the bat's ears. The closer the bat is to an object, the faster the bat sends out beeps. When a bat is far from an object, the bat sends out 5 beeps per second, but when the bat is close to the object, it may send out beeps at the rate of 200 per second.

3

1. A bird's feathers are made up of

   ○ bone. ○ dead cells. ○ hair. ○ cartilage.

2. Which of these birds uses its wings to fly underwater?

   ○ Hawk ○ Hummingbird ○ Crow ○ Penguin

3. The bird's skeleton has a stiff backbone to maintain a fixed position when the bird is

   ○ sleeping. ○ standing. ○ flying. ○ building nests.

4. The smallest birds are

   ○ sparrows. ○ canaries. ○ finches. ○ hummingbirds.

5. Hummingbirds get their name because of the sound they make with their

   ○ beak. ○ wings. ○ head. ○ voice.

6. The smallest hummingbird weighs less than

   ○ a penny. ○ a feather. ○ a spider web. ○ an ant.

7. The hummingbird's heart rate is

   ○ less than a hundred beats per minute.

   ○ less than one thousand beats per minute.

   ○ more than a thousand beats per minute.

   ○ more than two thousand beats per minute.

8. What is a big danger for the bee hummingbird?

   ○ Drowning

   ○ Getting caught in butterfly nets

   ○ Flying too high

   ○ Getting caught in a spider web

9. There are around _____ species of bats.

   ○ 16 ○ 20 ○ 900 ○ 1,800

10. The smallest bat weighs

    ○ less than a grain of sand.   ○ as much as a sparrow.

    ○ more than a penny.   ○ less than a penny.

11. Bats have

    ○ no eyes.   ○ eyes that cannot see.

    ○ eyes that can see.   ○ huge tongues.

12. To navigate at night, bats use

    ○ radar.   ○ echolalia.   ○ echolocation.   ○ sense of touch.

13. The wing of a bat looks like an arm with an enlarged

    ○ thumb.   ○ hand.   ○ finger.   ○ palm.

14. Which statement is not true?

    ○ Both bats and birds have wings.

    ○ Both birds and bats have eyes.

    ○ Both birds and bats are warm-blooded.

    ○ Both birds and bats are mammals.

15. A bat's wing is covered with

    ○ dead cells.   ○ feathers.   ○ skin.   ○ scales.

16. The largest bats have a wingspan of about

    ○ three pounds.   ○ six feet.   ○ 50 inches.   ○ two and a half feet.

Part 3

Number of errors [   ]

16 items

Point Charts

Lesson	Group Points A	B	Individual Points C	D	Bonus		TOTAL
1						=	
2						=	
3						=	
4						=	
5						=	

Lesson	Group Points A	B	Individual Points C	D	Bonus		TOTAL
26						=	
27						=	
28						=	
29						=	
30						=	

Lesson	Group Points A	B	Individual Points C	D	Bonus		TOTAL
6						=	
7						=	
8						=	
9						=	
10						=	

Lesson	Group Points A	B	Individual Points C	D	Bonus		TOTAL
31						=	
32						=	
33						=	
34						=	
35						=	

Lesson	Group Points A	B	Individual Points C	D	Bonus		TOTAL
11						=	
12						=	
13						=	
14						=	
15						=	

Lesson	Group Points A	B	Individual Points C	D	Bonus		TOTAL
36						=	
37						=	
38						=	
39						=	
40						=	

Lesson	Group Points A	B	Individual Points C	D	Bonus		TOTAL
16						=	
17						=	
18						=	
19						=	
20						=	

Lesson	Group Points A	B	Individual Points C	D	Bonus		TOTAL
41						=	
42						=	
43						=	
44						=	
45						=	

Lesson	Group Points A	B	Individual Points C	D	Bonus		TOTAL
21						=	
22						=	
23						=	
24						=	
25						=	

Lesson	Group Points A	B	Individual Points C	D	Bonus		TOTAL
46						=	
47						=	
48						=	
49						=	
50						=	

Point Charts

Lesson	Group Points A	B	Individual Points C	D	Bonus		TOTAL
51						=	
52						=	
53						=	
54						=	
55						=	

Lesson	Group Points A	B	Individual Points C	D	Bonus		TOTAL
56						=	
57						=	
58						=	
59						=	
60						=	

Lesson	Group Points A	B	Individual Points C	D	Bonus		TOTAL
61						=	
62						=	
63						=	
64						=	
65						=	

Lesson	Group Points A	B	Individual Points C	D	Bonus		TOTAL
66						=	
67						=	
68						=	
69						=	
70						=	

Lesson	Group Points A	B	Individual Points C	D	Bonus		TOTAL
71						=	
72						=	
73						=	
74						=	
75						=	

Lesson	Group Points A	B	Individual Points C	D	Bonus		TOTAL
76						=	
77						=	
78						=	
79						=	
80						=	

Lesson	Group Points A	B	Individual Points C	D	Bonus		TOTAL
81						=	
82						=	
83						=	
84						=	
85						=	

Lesson	Group Points A	B	Individual Points C	D	Bonus		TOTAL
86						=	
87						=	
88						=	
89						=	
90						=	

Lesson	Group Points A	B	Individual Points C	D	Bonus		TOTAL
91						=	
92						=	
93						=	
94						=	
95						=	

Lesson	Group Points A	B	Individual Points C	D	Bonus		TOTAL
96						=	
97						=	
98						=	
99						=	
100						=	

Point Charts

Lesson	Group Points A	B	Individual Points C	D	Bonus		TOTAL
101						=	
102						=	
103						=	
104						=	
105	█					=	

Lesson	Group Points A	B	Individual Points C	D	Bonus		TOTAL
116						=	
117						=	
118						=	
119						=	
120	█					=	

Lesson	Group Points A	B	Individual Points C	D	Bonus		TOTAL
106						=	
107						=	
108						=	
109						=	
110	█					=	

Lesson	Group Points A	B	Individual Points C	D	Bonus		TOTAL
121						=	
122						=	
123						=	
124						=	
125	█					=	

Lesson	Group Points A	B	Individual Points C	D	Bonus		TOTAL
111						=	
112						=	
113						=	
114						=	
115	█					=	

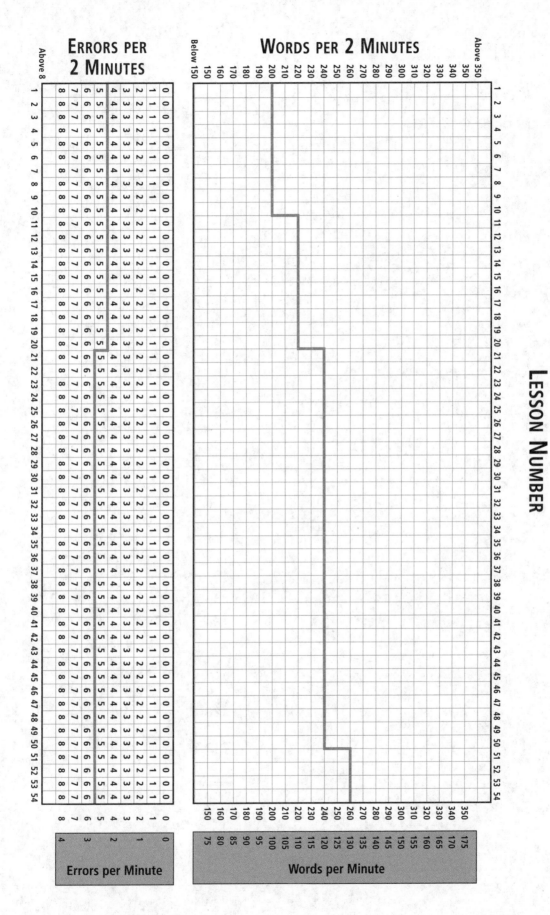

Individual Reading Progress Chart

Decoding C: LESSONS 1–54

LESSON NUMBER

Errors per Minute

4 3 2 1 0

Words per Minute

75 80 85 90 95 100 105 110 115 120 125 130 135 140 145 150 155 160 165 170 175

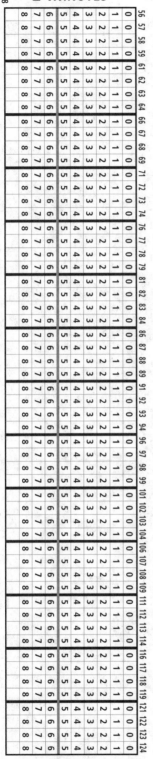

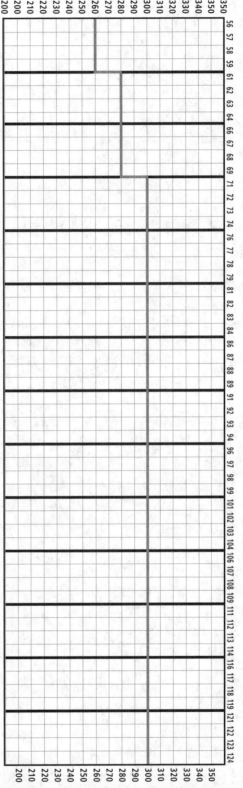